PAUL RAMSEY

Deeds and Rules
in Christian Ethics

Scottish Journal of Theology Occasional Papers No. 11

DEEDS AND RULES IN
CHRISTIAN ETHICS

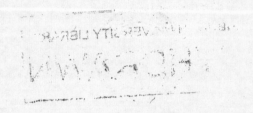

DEEDS AND RULES IN CHRISTIAN ETHICS

by
PAUL RAMSEY

Scottish Journal of Theology Occasional Papers
No. 11

OLIVER AND BOYD
EDINBURGH: TWEEDDALE COURT
LONDON: 39A WELBECK STREET W.1

FIRST PUBLISHED . . . 1965

PUBLISHED BY OLIVER AND BOYD LTD.
FOR THE SCOTTISH JOURNAL OF THEOLOGY LTD.
AND PRINTED BY ROBERT CUNNINGHAM AND SONS LTD., ALVA

CONTENTS

CONTENTS

INTRODUCTION

Iᴛ is the fashion today to speak of certain dons or professors as men who 'do' philosophy or 'do' ethics. This manner of speaking is itself very revealing, since it suggests the separation of a thinker's being from his doing. It suggests the triumph, at the very heart of philosophy in the contemporary period, of technical reason or mental action over a philosopher's concern in his being for being itself and truth itself. Has there not occurred in our time a severe contraction of 'the range of reason', and a reduction of the life of the mind to the doing of propositional puzzles? To this, the definition of philosophy as the love of wisdom, and as not the doing of anything at all, seems infinitely to be preferred.

Nevertheless, I shall adopt this manner of speaking in this essay on the method or methods of Christian ethics, and ask: How are we to *do* Christian ethics?

A leading thinker in the United States who engages in the doing of ethics is Professor William K. Frankena of the University of Michigan. He has modestly challenged Christian theologians to say more clearly what they mean to be doing when they are doing Christian ethics. Since evidently he reads us and has endeavoured to come to clarity about the meaning of many of the contemporary treatises in this genre, he deserves an answer. Moreover, the formulation of his question to Christian ethicists may serve to organise or reorganise the questions we think we are asking and answering about the nature of the Christian life. His formulation of the issue may also help to bring to some conclusion, or to an end, some of the confused and fruitless debates that are going on between the 'old' and the 'new' morality.

As with the question: How should we be *doing* Christian ethics?, I shall adopt Frankena's terminology purely as a *heuristic* device in order to discover, if possible, the proper method or methods of Christian ethics. Perhaps there are better terms in which to proceed with this inquiry, or it may be that Frankena's terms should in the end be replaced by a better formulation. But first we ought to see how far they will take us.

Christian ethics proposes that the basic norm and the distinctive character of the Christian life is Christian love (*agapé*). If other ethics rests upon a concept of moral duty (*deontology*) or upon a goal to be achieved (*teleology*), Christian ethics finds its basis in *agapé*. The fundamental question concerning the Christian life is whether from *agapé* there comes any instruction concerning the moral life, or any formative influence productive of a Christian style of life. And the basic question concerning Christian ethics is whether agapism is a third type of normative theory beside the ethics of duty and the ethics of goal-seeking.

The strength of Frankena's book on *Ethics*[1] is that he gets beyond meta-ethics and the analysis of moral language and takes up the question of normative ethics; and it is an additional strength that the author does not promptly reduce Christian ethics either to deontology or to utilitarianism. Instead he seems open to the persuasion that Christian ethics offers a distinct type of normative theory. 'It may be', he writes, 'that we must regard pure agapism as a third kind of normative theory in addition to deontological and teleological ones.' If not, it has already been covered by these types and Christian theologians may as well admit it, even if there may be some religious or emotional values still to be gained from continuing to use religious words for the very same norms which philosophers comprehend in other terms when they do ethics.

Then Professor Frankena points out that if Christian ethics is a possible theory of normative ethics it may or will or must take two forms, which he calls *act-agapism* and *rule-agapism*. These are the two possible views of how Christian love best exhibits itself in practice.

Act-agapism, says Frankena, holds that we are never to appeal to rules. Instead, 'we are to tell what we should do in a particular situation simply by getting clear about the facts of that situation and then asking what is the loving or the most loving thing to do in it. In other words, we are to apply the law of love directly and separately in each case with which we are confronted.'

Rule-agapism, by contrast, seeks 'to determine what we

[1] Englewood Cliffs, New Jersey: Prentice-Hall, 1963. The following quotations are from pp. 43-44.

ought to do, not by asking which *act* is the most loving, but by determining which *rules of action* are most love embodying . . .'.

In proposing that these are the two different forms which Christian ethics may take, Frankena uses terms drawn from the current debates among philosophical ethicists who have long been accustomed to speak of 'act-utilitarianism' and 'rule-utilitarianism'. Theologians these days have a professional allergy against 'rules'; and they will object to our using, even provisionally, Frankena's formulation in a discussion of the method or methods and types of Christian ethics. But surely it would be sheer emotionalism to object to the word 'rule', simply because it is habitual to philosophers and strange, even offensive, to theologians. It should also be remembered that I am using the word only as a heuristic device to see how far it will take us toward discoveries ahead. If 'rule' proves finally unusable for the purposes of Christian ethics, another word will have to be found—perhaps 'principle', 'middle axiom', 'ideal', 'directive', 'guidance', 'orders', 'ordinances', the 'structures' of *agapé* or of *koinonia* life, the 'style' of the Christian life, or the 'anatomy' or 'pattern' of Christian responsibility.

Another objection will be directed against the coining of such a jargon-word as 'agapism'; and, more important, against Frankena's seeming limitation of constructive Christian ethics to the *agapé* school of theologians. Here, however, we ought not to be distracted from the more important point Frankena addresses to Christian ethicists. The same two options remain in Christian ethics, no matter what term is used to replace *agapé* in indicating the reality upon which the Christian life rests. The Christian life may still take two forms: it may be productive of *acts only* or of *rules also*.

For example, if Christian ethics is *koinonia* (community)-ethics and if this can be demonstrated to be in any way different from *agapé*-ethics, then some Christian moralists in elaborating the ethics of the Christian community (the ethics of *koinonia*) will affirm that we are to tell what we should do in a particular situation simply by getting clear about the facts of that situation and then asking what is the fellowship-creating or the most fellowship-creating thing to do. Others will affirm that we are to determine what we ought to do by determining which *rules of action* are the most fellowship-creating or most aligned with the *koinonia* God is creating through his work with men. Thus

3

there may be an act-*koinonia* ethics and a rule-*koinonia* ethics. The same decision must be made if any other term is believed to be the illuminating one to use in an analysis of the ethical reality beneath the Christian life.

Now, no philosopher who is an act-utilitarian would think of making his case by simply accusing the rule-utilitarian of having abandoned the principle of utility. He would not charge, at the beginning of the argument and to avoid any contest, that the rule-utilitarian is not applying the test of utility in his ethics, or that utility is any less the sovereign and the sole sovereign over right conduct, or that the lordship of utility has been weakened and divided where there are any utility-embodying rules. Nor would a rule-utilitarian stoop to conquer the act-utilitarian by calling him a 'relativist' or a 'subjectivist'. It remained for theologians to invent these un-logics, in the debate (which as a consequence never ensues) between act-agapism or act-*koinonia* ethics and rule-agapism or rule-*koinonia* ethics.

The real issue is whether there are any *agapé*- or *koinonia*-embodying rules; and, if there are, what these rules may be. Theologians today are simply deceiving themselves and playing tricks with their readers when they pit the freedom and ultimacy of *agapé* (or covenant-obedience, or *koinonia*, or community, or any other primary theological or ethical concept) against rules, without asking whether *agapé* can and may or must work through rules and embody itself in certain principles which are regulative or the guidance of practice.

I seriously suggest that Frankena's analysis fits the issues now very much in debate among theological ethicists; and that to employ his clarifying terminology will remove some of the acrimony from these debates and help us get on with the doing of Christian ethics—or, if you prefer, it may help us better to clarify the church's proclamation in its relation to moral problems. For one thing, a rule-agapist should no longer accuse the act-agapist of being a 'materialist', a 'relativist', or 'subjectivist' or a compromiser when he is only an act-agapist. And the proponent of Christian 'situational-ethics' should no longer accuse the proponent of rule-agapism of being a 'legalist' lacking in 'compassion' when he only believes that Christian compassion can and may and must embody itself in certain rules of action.

4

Once this is understood to be the issue at stake, I also contend that it can be shown that a proper understanding of the moral life will be one in which Christians determine what we ought to do in very great measure by determining which rules of action are most love-embodying, but that there are also always situations in which we are to tell what we should do by getting clear about the facts of that situation and then asking what is the loving or the most loving thing to do in it. The latter may even be at work in every case of the creative casuistry of in-principled love going into action. But it will be an instance of thoughtlessness or sentimentality if any Christian in the conduct of his life or any theologian in the doing of Christian ethics seeks to overleap or avoid his responsibility for determining whether there are any love-embodying rules of action, and what these rules may be.

ON TAKING SEXUAL RESPONSIBILITY
SERIOUSLY ENOUGH

THE 'essay by a group of Friends' entitled *Towards a Quaker View of Sex*[1] reached profoundly into the question whether there are any rules of action embodying Christian responsibility in sexual behaviour, or whether there are only acts that embody such responsibility. But then it flinched and drew back from the conclusion to which argument itself was about to lead—indeed, to which it had led. This document provides, therefore, a significant 'case study' in how we should understand the meaning of *Christian* responsibility, or the *Christian* meaning of responsibility. From an examination of this pamphlet we may learn how to do and how not to do Christian ethics.

When is it right for intercourse to take place? asked the Quakers.

> It should *not* happen until the partners come to know each other so well that the sexual contact becomes a consummation, a deeply meaningful total expression of a friendship in which each has accepted the other's reality and shared the other's interests.[2]

If that is when *not*, when *should* it?

In these Friends' answer to this question, *responsibility embodied in the act* reached the border where it had to become *responsibility embodied in a general rule*. Let us shorten these terms, and say that a crucial choice in Christian ethics is between act-responsibility and rule-responsibility. We can also say that these Friends reached the border where *Christian love embodied in an act* had to become *Christian love embodied in a general rule*, or where act-agapism, fully explored, was about to be replaced by rule-agapism:

> Could we say also that at least in spirit each should be committed to the other—should be open to the other in heart and mind? This would mean that each cared deeply about what might happen to the other and would do everything possible to

[1] Friends Home Service Committee, Friends House, Euston Road, London, 1963.   [2] p. 45.

6

meet the other's needs and lessen any suffering that had to be faced. It would mean a willingness to accept responsibility. . . .

Should not there also be a commitment to a shared view of the nature and purpose of life?[1]

Why not affirm all this, reminiscent as these words are of the marriage vow? Precisely because they are. Precisely because that would be a rule or a pattern embodying responsibility. Therefore, these Friends say:

At once we are aware that this is to ask for nothing less than the full commitment of marriage, indeed most marriages begin with a much less adequate basis.[2]

Thus the question of the meaning of responsibility in sexual ethics was simply begged in behalf of act-agapism or act-responsibility. Some such words might still be used as a 'challenge' to sexual acts within marriage and to sexual acts outside of marriage, but we cannot 'legislate' or 'draw clear lines between good and evil', not even when an ethics of responsibility was probed to the point, and beyond the point, of drawing them.

Clearly, one cannot explore the meaning of Christian responsibility very profoundly without suddenly finding himself discussing, in this connexion, the moral meaning of *marriage* itself. He will therefore find himself discussing *marital* relations, and not *pre*-marital relations. In making a judgment upon all this, a Christian has first to remind himself in no uncertain terms that the Christian view of sex and of marriage never was a theology of the marriage *ceremony*. Ours is not the task of defending bourgeois respectability or legal paper or church ceremonies and registers. None of these things have anything to do with defining a pre-marital or a conjugal relation. The man and the woman marry each other in fact when their consents are the response to and the responsibility for each other's reality which these Friends describe. Sexual consummation is then the consummation of an existing marriage, whether or not they have ever been—as we err in saying—'married'.

This is acknowledged both in the sphere of the State and in the sphere of the Church. In most state jurisdictions in the United States, one can get married according to all the regula-

[1] p. 45.   [2] p. 45.

tions of the 20-odd volumes of the state's marriage law or he can get married without them. This is provided by the last paragraph on the last page of Vol. 20, which usually states: 'None of the foregoing is intended to abolish the common law', i.e. the unwritten law that lets people alone to make their marriages simply out of their will to be responsible to and for one another. (The rules of evidence that can later establish that they did this need not be brought into the question.) If it is judged desirable to legislate the omnicompetence of *legal* marriage, it is necessary for the legislature to enact a written law abolishing a 'law' that was never written.

And in the sacrament of marriage in the Roman church, the parties are the priests administering the sacrament to one another (if only they are baptised and if their consents are as responsible as their words say). When the Council of Trent wanted to prohibit 'clandestine marriages' (which were not 'secret' but ordinary Christian sacramental marriages brought into being without a priest), it touched the sacrament co-donated by the two only by requiring a priest as witness. For 150 years after Trent 'surprise marriages' were valid and not infrequent in France. A man and a woman simply accosted a priest on the street and quickly said in his presence words expressive of their consenting to take one another responsibly. Thereafter, the priest could not deny that a marriage had taken place in his presence.

It is a matter of indifference that the summary words 'wife' and 'husband' or other words have to be used to prove common law marriage or to perform the sacrament of marriage, rather than the more extended statement of responsibility written by these Friends.

After seeing clearly what makes a marriage and the only morally important distinction between pre- and post-marital intercourse, if then anyone still wants to defend the need of a civil or religious ceremony he will have to do this for practical reasons that are ethically rather insignificant, if indeed they are not entirely non-moral. He will have somehow to link an ethic of responsibility in love with the need for practical, public tests of this. He will have to say with Peter Bertocci, who *connects* but does not confuse legal marriage with the moral meaning of the responsible love that makes marriage, when he writes:

> In marrying they are saying that they wish others, both those who love them and all others on whom their activities impinge, to hold them responsible for a certain level of conduct. . . . The very fact that marriage does involve problems which lovers are not sure they can yet accept means that more is involved and more is to be demanded than the values of sexual love. . . . A love which is too narrow to accept the legal responsibility for the other person, and a love which blinds two persons to the community's need for the *kind of love* which will accept the fullest responsibility for the lives of others, is not all that love can be.[1]

They may, of course, need some such external test simply to know whether what they are talking about as lovers is the question of *pre*-marital relations and not actually, in the ethical sense, a question only of their marital relations, or the consummation of their marriage. However important legalities and ceremonies may be, they are only external checks which exhibit to others the fact that the lovers are married, and which may help the lovers themselves to be steadfast in the responsible resolve which alone made them married.

But these Friends drew back when they saw that to ask what they were driven to ask from within the interior of an ethics of responsibility was 'to ask nothing less than the full commitment of marriage'. They chose act-responsibility when a rule of action embodying responsibility appeared on the horizon and was obviously required by their own analysis.

For the Friends to return to acts only, required a lessening or weakening of their ethics of responsibility. It required less than the fullest response for them to reopen the question of genuinely pre-marital relations after that question had been closed by the emergence of full commitment to the other person's reality in what amounted to marriage. This is an interesting demonstration of the fact that act-responsibility can be established only by arbitrarily rejecting rule-responsibility once the rule of action embodying responsibility has been seen to flow from within sensitive reflection upon the moral life itself.

So the authors of the Quaker essay draw back from clarity about sexual responsibility. They choose rather a twilight zone where (according to their own description of human experience in this zone) not all is responsibility or full response. 'A deliberate intention to avoid responsibility' is, of course, ruled out.

---

[1] 'Towards a Christian View of Sex Education', in Simon Doniger: *Sex and Religion Today*. New York: Association Press, 1953, pp. 178-9.

CE B

(Even that is some sort of rule-morality!) But for irresponsibility to be absent, responsibility need not be present. Only in this twilight does act-responsibility again become possible for Christian conscience. The words now justifying the act are 'openness' to and a 'seed' or 'measure' of what was before under consideration:

> Where there is genuine tenderness, an openness to responsibility, and the seed of commitment, God is surely not shut out. Can we not say that God can enter any relationship in which there is a measure of selfless love?[1]

I suppose that no Christian since Augustine has denied that God is there where there is any measure or beauty or order or seed or any being at all!

At another place in the pamphlet, the authors reach down to something even less a measure or seed of responsibility, and far more 'wayward', in order to exclude as 'unrealistic' a rule of behaviour embodying *agapé*-responsibility that was proposed by Sherwin Bailey.[2]

> He [Bailey] holds that to say 'I love you' means nothing less than this: 'I want you, just as you are, to share the whole of my life, and I ask you to take me, just as I am, to share the whole of your life'. He further says that it ought never to be said unless marriage is possible, right, and at the time of speaking intended. That such a statement is unrealistic is at the root of our work.[3]

One would have thought that whether a rule of right conduct is realistic is not the first or the main point to be proven. Even so, what the Quakers refer to in order to refute Bailey is not acts that are governed by a measure or seed of responsibility but instead the conviction, drawn from 'the actual experiences of people', that

> love cannot be confined to a pattern. The waywardness of love is part of its nature and this is both its glory and its tragedy. If love did not tend to leap every barrier, if it could be tamed, it would not be the tremendous creative power we know it to be and want it to be.[4]

There are, therefore, two steps by which these Friends withdraw from an analysis of the entire meaning of responsibility. First, they withdraw from full to only a measured responsibility (and this is correlated with flinching from rule-responsibility

---

[1] p. 45.
[2] *Common Sense about Sexual Ethics*, London: S.C.M. Press, 1962, p. 116.
[3] p. 39.   [4] p. 39.

10

and an acceptance of act-responsibility in their underlying moral theory). Secondly, they bring into prominence love's asserted tendency to go further down the slope or up into the heights; and they substitute for even a measure or seed of responsibility in action love's own waywardness, its untame-ability, and the glory and tragedy of wanting to leap every barrier and escape every pattern.

If sincere Christian people including theological ethicists can be found simply refusing to take responsibility seriously enough when rules of action, and not acts alone, threaten to emerge from this, is it to be expected that adolescent boys and girls will take any measure of sexual act-responsibility seriously? Was the editorial comment upon this Quaker document by the Jesuit weekly *America* (20th April 1963) altogether wrong:

> In plain English, they mean that it is right for two kids to commit fornication if they *really* love each other. . . . If the sex act is only an act of love and not, in the intention of God and nature, an act of generation, there is no reason why people should not make it a gesture comparable to a kiss.

I do not mean that the only way to avoid this conclusion is to affirm, with Roman Catholics, that an act of sexual love is *primarily* a procreative act. But if we Protestants take the view that sexual love is primarily an act of union between the man and the woman, then this viewpoint may still take two forms: act-union and rule-union.

Nor do I assert that an ethics of act-union is at once to be accused of being 'a purely subjective evaluation of the rightness and wrongness of sexual relationship' (as *America* said of the Quaker statement). Nevertheless, it may be that rules of action are to be found in an ethics of sexual love *qua* unitative; and this ought not *prima facie* to be excluded, as so often happens today among those who pride themselves on knowing all about the sexual revolution and who want to be compassionate or who only contemplate the 'situation'.

An act-personalism or an act-responsibilism or an act-agapism or act-*koinonia* (community) ethics or an act-unitive sex ethic is not a subjective vagary. It is simply wrong. Marriage as a rule of action embodying everything that Christian re-sponsibility means in sexual life may be defined as the mutual and exclusive exchange of the right to acts that of themselves tend to establish and to nourish unity of life between the partners. The fact that Christian ethics knows this to be the truth about sexual responsibility ought not to be withheld from young people, no matter how much sexual behaviour may be in revolution.

Somewhat contradicting the complete waywardness of human sexual love, these Friends report:

> from the intimate experience of several of us, that it is possible to give substance to the traditional code, to live within its requirements, enriched by an experience of love at its most generous and tender, and conscious of our debt to Christ in showing us what love implies.[1]

If Christ shows us what love implies, and if this comes not only from an experience of love at its most generous and tender, it may be asked why we are not obliged to affirm that the (so-called) traditional code contains rules of action that simply embody Christian responsibility when this is full and strong?

The reason given for *not* affirming this is 'the awareness that the traditional code, in itself, does not come from the heart'. Yet the experience of living within its requirements did come from the heart, and from these Friends' debt to Christ in showing them what love implies. Actually, underneath their rejection of 'the traditional code, in itself', is the human heart in the modern, post-Christian age. Undoubtedly, it is the case that 'for the great majority of men and women it has no roots in feeling or true conviction' today.

Christian ethics must certainly be able to do more than to take note of this fact, else there is no hope of restoring any sort of Christian *ethos* to the churches in the modern age, let alone the world at large. It can certainly be demonstrated that, historically speaking, the traditional code, in itself, came from the human heart as men were taught by Christ what love implied. The theologian is blinded and in error if he imagines that from Ephesians 5 came only an act-agapism and not the rule-agapism which established in the mind of Christendom its laws of marriage—elevating, for example, Roman contractual marriage into the full measure of the requirements of steadfast covenant. And he is a poor constructive ethicist who, without much argumentation, rules out the possibility that rules of action may still be fashioned by hearts instructed by Christ to know what love itself implies.

[1] p. 41.

That was a profoundly penetrating remark of Professor Tom F. Driver who launched the discussion of this Quaker statement among American Protestants[1] upon the quandary of the ministry in face of the hearts of modern men:

> ... When traditional religious authority is not felt by a man to be binding upon his conscience, then it is not possible to preach to him the Law and the Gospel at the same time. Well aware of the disasters created by preaching the Law only, ministers tend to say more about the Gospel. But in the long run this has the effect of undermining the Law itself, at least in so far as the Law must be spelled out as a specific rule of conduct.

Why not, for once, try the preaching of 'the Gospel contained in this Law', the law of marriage as a rule embodying Christian responsible action?

The fact that this is not done, and today can scarcely be done, requires explanation. It is due to the erosion of Christian substance from our churches, from the ministry, from theological ethics itself. This, in turn, explains the question-begging prejudice in favour of act-agapism or act-responsibility ethics, or else the prejudice in favour of a merely situational ethics explains the erosion of Christian ethical substance. Which, it is difficult to tell.

One final and exceedingly important point must be mentioned in this discussion of the Quaker pamphlet as a 'case study' in how to do and how not to do Christian ethics. Taking Christian ethics with utmost seriousness requires that we consider the importance of the *ethos*, the social habits, the customs and laws of any society—whether this be church or civil society. In the foregoing, we have asked whether individual responsibility is embodied in acts only or also in general rules of conduct. Now, we must ask whether there are any *societal* rules that embody the highest general responsibility and which are the most fellowship-producing rules for society as a whole, or whether this is a matter of 'situational' acts only.

The Quaker essay notes that

> *there must be a morality of some sort to govern sexual relationships.* An experience so profound in its effect upon people and upon the community cannot be left wholly to private judgment. It will never be right for two people to say to each other 'We'll do what we want, and what happens between us is nobody else's business.'

[1] 'Taking Sex Seriously', *Christianity and Crisis*, 14th October 1963.

13

However private an act it is never without its impact on society, and we must never behave as though society—which includes our other friends—did not exist.[1]

How can Christians nourish the seeds of a wider social responsibility while seeming to praise only acts and never rules that embody personal responsibility between the two parties to sexual relations? Plainly, the waywardness of the human heart works against any *ethos*, customs or laws that are generally good for all, and not only against 'the traditional code'. Protestant Christian ethics is often too profoundly personal to be ethically relevant, if in this is included even a minimum of concern for the social habits and customs of a people. Ordinarily, we do not take Christian ethics with enough seriousness to illumine the path men, women *and society* should follow today. This suggests that only some form of rule-agapism, and not act-agapism, can be consistent with the elaboration of a Christian's social responsibilities. No social morality ever was founded, or ever will be founded, upon a situational ethic.[2]

[1] p. 40.

[2] When the foregoing was first published in *Christianity and Crisis*, 6th January 1964, the most intelligent letter the Editor received understood my quarrel with the Quakers to be 'an example of the permanent quarrel between the legalistic and the compassionate approach to problems of human conduct', though the writer did go on to remark upon 'the fruitfulness of this permanent quarrel when both sides are maintained with a good courage' (*C. & C.*, 17th February 1964). What did that writer take *agapé* or Christian compassion to mean? In this sentimental age when disciplined reflection seems not to be wanted even in the doing of Christian ethics, it is all but impossible to persuade anyone of this very simple point: supposing the Christian life to be founded on compassion alone, this may still take two forms: it may be productive of acts only or of rules also. One has to *prove* in Christian ethical theory that we are to tell what we should do in a particular situation simply by getting clear about the facts of that situation and then asking what is the compassionate or the most compassionate thing to do, no less than one has to prove in Christian ethical theory that we are to determine what we ought to do by determining which rules of action are most compassion-embodying. Calling the rule-agapist by the name of 'legalist' or the act-agapist by such names as 'relativist' or 'subjectivist' gets us nowhere, no matter how edifying it feels to fling around the word 'compassion'.

THE HONEST TO GOD
IN FOR CHRIST'S SAKE DEBATE

IN Great Britain theological professors and 'professors' of the faith seem to take one another seriously; and, moreover, they do theological work on the unusual premise that a theological position may have practical import for the life of the church and of the individual Christian. As a consequence, a spate of articles, pamphlets and volumes came out in response to Bishop John A. T. Robinson's *Honest to God* and to the essays in *Soundings*, edited by A. R. Vidler.[1] It was to be expected that theological issues should receive first attention, and that only afterward was a rumbling of drums called forth by the smoke signals sent up about 'the new morality'.

If I may be permitted to intervene in this discussion it would be to say that there needs to be imposed upon it some order and conceptual clarity; and that until this is done, by protagonist and antagonist alike, only 'dialogue' and word-play or word-weapons can result, and never a conclusion from the whole debate or from either of the sides who do not seem fully to grasp what is being proposed or opposed. What Bishop Robinson has written on theology, liturgy and prayer seems to me far more significant and worthy of attention than what he has written on Christian ethics. Perhaps this impression is due to the fact that he knows more about those subjects than I do. In any case, he does not seem yet to have said clearly what he means to say about Christian morality. Without a firmer, analytical grasp on the position he means to expound, Robinson will not be able to be grasped, and rightly grappled with.

On first reading Robinson, one's attention will be drawn to the contentions into which he packs the most intellectual passion, and to passages where he verges on sensational illustra-

---

[1] J. A. T. Robinson: *Honest to God*, London: S.C.M. Press, 1963; A. R. Vidler, ed.: *Soundings*, Cambridge: The University Press, 1962; A. R. Vidler, ed.: *Objections to Christian Belief*, Philadelphia and New York: J. B. Lippincott Co., 1964; Michael Ramsey: *Image Old and New*, London: S.P.C.K., 1963; Eric Mascall: *Up and Down in Adria*, London: The Faith Press, 1963; Alan Richardson, ed.: *Four Anchors from the Stern*, London: S.C.M. Press, 1963. [The last two titles are taken from Acts 27.27-29.]

tions of Christian freedom. From this one might suppose that Robinson is only an act-agapist (or call it what you will). He is certainly not a subjectivist or a relativist or a giver-in to the current moral laxity or an apostate from the ethical insights once delivered to the saints. Yet he is an ambiguous proponent of act-agapism. He does not always say that the Christian is to tell what he should do simply by getting the facts clear and asking which *actions* best embody love. This is, of course, his central theme; but this is not all he means to say concerning the Christian life.

Robinson's voice is the voice of pure act-agapism, but his hands are the hands of rule-agapism (cf. Genesis 27.22). We shall have to ask what is the relation between his voice and the skins of the kids and the goats upon his hands and upon the smooth of his neck; and where in fact he got those skins and the goodly garments of Rebekah's elder son (cf. Genesis 27.15). We shall have to ask for an account of the rule-agapism which holds pride of second place in his system; and what coherence there is between this and the utterances of a seemingly pure act-agapism. Then and only then will we properly grasp Robinson's writings on Christian morality, and be able to prove their insufficiency or their incoherence as a constructive statement of Christian ethics. This will be my second illustration of the illuminating and heuristic power of Frankena's setting of the terms for Christian theories of normative ethics.

The act-agapism is plain to see. According to Robinson the ultimate norm requires us 'to open oneself to another *unconditionally* in love', or to meet 'the unconditional in the conditioned in unconditional personal relationship.'[1] Jesus' proclamation of the Kingdom of God announced not the Year nor even the Day but the Moment of the Lord. His parables and teachings were 'illustrations of what love may *at any moment* require of anyone'.[2] We are to be men for others as Jesus Christ was 'the man for others'. This means 'having no absolutes but his love, being totally uncommitted in every other respect but totally committed in this'. It means 'accepting as the basis of moral judgments the actual concrete relationship in all its particularity . . .'.[3] Love alone is the standard because love has 'a built-in moral compass' enabling it to 'home'

[1] *Honest to God*, pp. 99, 105. [2] ibid., pp. 110-11 (italics added).
[3] ibid., p. 114.

intuitively upon the need of the other (note well!) in the singleness of the moment of encounter with him. This is 'an ethic of radical responsiveness'[1]; in short, an ethic of pure act-*agapé*. 'Love's casuistry' is summed up in Joseph Fletcher's rephrasing of St. Augustine's *dilige et quod vis fac*: 'love and *then* what you will, do'.[2]

There is nothing wrong with any of these statements except their two silent, unexamined assumptions: (1) that Christian love has in itself no *breadth* to match its personal depth and therefore no rule-implying power, and (2) that love 'homes' in only upon *the moment* in the neighbour's reality, for which it cares. This may explain why, when writing in this vein, Robinson finds it impossible to conceive that there may be a *moral bond* between persons (e.g. marriage) and not only an act-response or responsibility renewed every moment. The church's teachings on marriage seem to him either to bespeak the external commands of a God 'up' or 'out there'; or to furnish the world with metaphysical or quasi-physical 'occult realities'.[3] Perhaps the Bishop of Woolwich should learn from St. Augustine what St. Augustine learned from the Platonists, namely, how to *conceive*, how even to *think*, of spiritual substance or a spiritual bond that may be all the more real because it is not a 'quasi-physical' or 'occult' *thing*.

Pure act-agapism continues to be expressed in Bishop Robinson's recent book, *Christian Morals Today*,[4] where however this is interspersed with much else. In fact, there is so much rule-agapism or some other source of principles and directives set forth in this volume that one must demand that the author say where he got these goodly garments and skins in which to clothe personal encounter, or whence he thinks the Christian derives them. Still the asserted momentary *freedom of agapé* (which often seems to mean love's *inability* to bind itself in any way other than in acts that are the response of depth to depth) is never withdrawn.

This, of course, cannot be demonstrated by statements which

---

[1] ibid., p. 115.
[2] ibid., p. 119; Joseph Fletcher, 'The New Look in Christian Ethics', *Harvard Divinity Bulletin*, October 1959, p. 10. In my *Basic Christian Ethics* (New York: Charles Scribner's Sons, 1950), I expressed this as: 'Love, and do as you *then* please.' However, we shall see that doing everything that love requires, everything without a single exception, may include more than single acts.
[3] ibid., pp. 107, 108.
[4] London: S.C.M. Press and Philadelphia, Penn.: The Westminster Press, 1964.

only assert the sole *primacy* of love (which rule-agapism would also affirm). It cannot be demonstrated by Robinson's 'treating persons as persons with unconditional seriousness'[1]; nor by his statement that 'the most searching demands of pure personal relationship' is 'the basis of *all* moral judgments'[2] (since moral judgments may include judgments also concerning rules of action and need not concern acts only); nor even by his 'persons matter more, imponderably more, than any principles'[3] (since the question at issue is whether there are principles that embody love for persons or only acts of radical responsiveness to them).

Still, pure act-agapism seems still to be Robinson's point of view. This becomes clear, first, in the description of the 'inductive approach' to moral questions: 'The ends are not prescribed, the answers are not settled beforehand. But this is only to say that a real *decision* is involved in any responsible moral choice.'[4]

Pure act-agapism seems evident, secondly, in that rather a-gnostic discussion of 'the morality of involvement and discovery', 'searching out a satisfactory moral basis for personal life and for society'.[5] Here the premium is placed on a searching that never arrives at any answers, or at only quite provisional ones governing still questing acts of involvement. Here stress is emphatically placed on the seeming hypocrisy of Christians who join humanists, who are deeply impressed by the impenetrable mystery of moral existence, and go on a moral slumming expedition with them but in the belief that Christians know in advance that certain things are always wrong. The Christian should go in search of a presence, not a proposition. 'The Christian *goes in* trusting that God is always *in the situation before him* and that if and as he genuinely gives himself in love he will find God—for God is Love; and if he serves people, with no thought for them but as persons, he will discover himself ministering to Christ.'[6]

---

[1] ibid., pp. 36-37. [2] ibid., p. 8. [3] ibid., p. 42.

[4] ibid., p. 41. I would find proof of pure act-agapism in Robinson's statement, concerning his own children, that he 'would much rather give them the built-in moral values to use the freedom creatively . . .' (p. 44), except for the fact that the expression 'moral values' leaves it uncertain whether this means only *instant agapé* with its built-in moral compass zeroing in upon a personal encounter or may mean other values implied in or the fruit of *agapé*, or values derived from some other source.

[5] ibid., p. 39, quoting James Hemming, 'Moral Education in Chaos', in *New Society*, September 1963.

[6] ibid., pp. 38-39 (italics added).

It might be remarked that this is a good deal to know when setting out on pilgrimage; and that (to turn Robinson's argument on himself) the Christian who knows this might as well wait at the end of the road for his humanist brother to arrive there. Still, the theory of Christian normative ethics implied in this is pure act-agapism: the Christian life leads from love to love, and there are only situational acts in between.

Pure act-agapism seems evident, thirdly, from the remarks concerning sexual morality on the next to last page. I am inclined to treat this as something of a lapse after the amount and degree of better moral reasoning this book contains, and which we have yet to consider under the heading of rule-agapism and the questions to be raised about this. Still there it is, pretty clearly expressed. Robinson wants the present generation of youth to be 'genuinely free—to decide responsibly for themselves what love at its deepest really requires *of them*'. The author knows full well that a young girl may simply be 'the victim of emotional blackmail'—a susceptibility to which, indeed, our contemporary culture imposes on all young people because of its emphasis on romantic love as the sole determiner of meaningful acts. However subtle the dangers of mutual exploitation and the mutual violation of the humanity of the partners, Robinson at this point offers only an internal, attitudinal corrective. He joins with young people in a desire, which he may have first attributed to them, for 'a basis for morality that makes sense in terms of personal relationships'. 'They want *honesty* in sex', he writes 'as in everything else . . .. [Chastity] is honesty in sex; having physical relationships that *truthfully express* the degree of personal commitment that is there underneath.'[1]

To which it has to be said, very simply, that if the supreme criterion in Christian sexual morality is honesty and the truthful expression of personal commitment, such an ethic may still take either of two forms: act-honesty and act-truthfulness or rule-honesty and rule-truthfulness. These are merely shorthand expressions for saying that, on one view, a Christian tells

[1] ibid., p. 45. This is reminiscent of the passage in *Honest to God* (p. 119) which suggests that a man ask himself '*How much* do you love her?' and then 'accept *for himself* the decision that, if he doesn't, or doesn't very deeply, then his action is immoral, or if he does, then he will respect her far too much to use her or take liberties with her.' If there is only an inner, attitudinal question and an inner, attitudinal answer, then this *does* suggest that, if he does and does very deeply, then no matter what actions follow he does not use her or take liberties with her.

19

what he should do by asking only which act or acts best embodies personal honesty and truthfulness in sexual relations; while, on another view which assigns equal primacy to honesty in love as the sole norm, a Christian tells what he should do by asking whether there are any rules of conduct which best embody love, and if so what these rules may be.

So far the voice of Jacob.

Now let us direct attention to the goodly garments. To do so is to take up again the point at which we had arrived in discussing the Quaker document. It is to ask: What interpretation does Bishop Robinson give of societal rules of behaviour, customs and laws? What, indeed, is his view of the relation between the *agapé*-norm and those habitual excellencies of personal conduct (commonly called *virtues*) which make a man a dependable character in any social group, and without which he is good for nothing in love to God or neighbour?

There was already in the chapter on 'the new morality' in *Honest to God* a logical place for societal rules of action, whether these are to be understood to be among the utterances of love itself (rule-agapism) or to have been stolen from Esau and quite without uniquely Christian justification. Love's responses, Robinson wrote, 'may, and should, be hedged about by the laws and conventions of society, for these are the dykes of love in a wayward and loveless world'.[1] A Christian 'cannot but rely, in deep humility, upon guiding rules, upon the cumulative experience of one's own and other people's obedience. It is this bank of experience which gives us our working rules of "right" and "wrong", and without them we could not but flounder.'[2]

This requirement of a Christian social ethic is even more stressed by Robinson in his more recent *Christian Morals Today*.

> No person, no society, can continue or cohere for any length of time without an accepted ethic, just as ordered life becomes impossible without a recognised legal system or a stable economy. And the Christian least of all can be disinterested in these fields. The more he loves his neighbour, the more he will be concerned that the whole *ethos* of his society—cultural, moral, legal, political and economic—is a good one, preserving personality rather than destroying it.[3]

[1] *Honest to God*, p. 118.
[2] ibid., pp. 119-20.
[3] *Christian Morals Today*, p. 12.

A moral net there must be in any society. Christians must be to the fore in every age helping to construct it, criticise it, and keep it in repair.[1]

The deeper one's concern for persons, the more effectively one wants to see love buttressed by law.[2]

The foregoing quotations use not a few expressions, whether denotative or connotative, for what I call in this essay 'rules of action'. Concerning 'rules of action' the important question is not whether among them there are any that are generally and universally valid. That depressing question, or at least the paramount position assigned it, is more a product of the fear of certitude in a relativistic age than it is of anything else. There are really important questions to be clarified and settled before we modern men could give open-minded consideration to the possibility that there may be general rules of right conduct. It is significant that Robinson does not flinch as much as does the Quaker document from drawing a generally valid conclusion, and this will be pointed out in the sequel, along with the question how this comports either with his act-agapism or with his insistence upon having only 'working' rules when he is discussing rules at all. Still the fundamental question is whence come these rules and the ethical justification of them, whether they be generally or less than generally valid.

Are there rules of behaviour that are simply corollaries of the idea of covenant or of Christian love? Does *agapé* itself require elaboration in terms of those dispositional or character-traits catalogued by St. Paul as the works or fruits of the Spirit? Does the love of Christ for his church in-principle itself in terms of a very definite understanding of the conjugal love of man and wife and of the moral bond established by *agapé* between them? That would be rule-agapism.

Do the needed rules of action, the dykes and buttresses of love, simply arise in the mind's eye when Christians gaze steadily at the conditional—the particular situation in all its concreteness—in which they should display unconditional love for persons? Do Christian's simply make up the rules out of the lumber of the facts as a carpenter builds a table to serve some human need? Do the experiences they bank contain in themselves no moral meaning except as these are assumed into *agapé* and are shaped by it into patterns of action that vary

[1] ibid., p. 18. [2] ibid., p. 26.

21

indefinitely in the course of time and cultural change? That, too, would be a form of rule-agapism.

Do any of the rules of action with which *agapé* directs us to care for persons arise, not from the breadth and immanent wisdom of *agapé* itself or from the mere facts 'edified' so that they serve to buttress love in a loveless and wayward world, but from some other ethical justification than love itself alone supplies? Are the good garments, is the net and the dyke and are the laws of society and its conventions in any measure made of moral material that is not to be reduced to or found implied in Christian love? In addition to the standard that is distinctive and also primary in Christian ethics, are there any principles or sources of moral wisdom that while secondary and not distinctive are nevertheless necessary in a complete Christian theory of ethics? That would be agapism *mixed* with some other theory of normative ethics.[1] A *Christian* natural law theory would be an illustration of this possibility in Christian social ethics. But the category of mixed agapism ought not to be restricted to this example. *Any* notion of 'the orders' belongs to this classification. Presumably the three median types of Christian social outlook which H. Richard Niebuhr discusses[2] —'Christ above Culture' or the Catholic synthesis, 'Christ and Culture in Paradox' (e.g. Lutheranism), and 'Christ transforming Culture' (e.g. St Augustine, Calvinism, F. D. Maurice) —all find in the culture-pole some inherent if subordinate directives beyond the fact that, on these views, the love of Christ demands *that* the Christian assume an indeterminate responsibility for the culture and the social institutions in which men dwell.

I shall now undertake to collect, in some reasonable order, the various suggestions Bishop Robinson has made in answer to the questions that have just been raised. In doing so, I do not mean to imply that the different ways he seems to proceed from the *agapé*-centre in Christian ethics to an elaboration of additional directives are incompatible with one another. It seems, however, that these themes in his writings do require a drastic modification of the pure act-agapism to which he continues to give voice; and it *may* be that a choice will also have to be made between some of his different proposals concerning

---

[1] 'Mixed agapism' will be explained more fully in the final section of this paper.
[2] *Christ and Culture*, New York: Harper and Row, 1951.

how a Christian proceeds to the business of 'edifying' or borrowing rules of action.

1. *Polarity between Rules and Acts*

A first possibility is presented by the announced intention of the lectures on the 'old' and the 'new morality', published in *Christian Morals Today*. These terms refer to 'two starting-points', to a 'perennial polarity' in Christian ethics. They are 'not antithetical but complementary'. Between these perennially necessary poles there is a 'genuine dialectic', each is a 'corrective' of the other; 'one cannot be true at the expense of the other'.[1] An individual or a whole generation or culture may start at one end rather than at the other; but both are right and necessary. Each needs the emphasis that the other cherishes. These 'complementary rather than contradictory attempts to do justice to the great polarities which lie at the heart of the Christian ethic' ought never to become a 'sterile antagonism'.[2] There are only 'differences of "way in"' to certain abiding realities in Christian ethics which *all* Christians have an equal interest in holding in their proper, creative tension. . . . Neither side wishes to destroy that tension.'[3]

Since it is quite clear which 'way in', which pole, Bishop Robinson himself espouses, and which he believes to be the right or most illuminating way to do Christian ethics, or at least the right way in to be taken in this generation, there may be some slight question about whether these statements are to be taken with utmost seriousness. Is this one of Kierkegaard's pseudonyms speaking?

Still this is the announced perennial method of Christian ethics; and concerning it the following basic questions have to be asked: Whence come the goodly garments of the other pole? Are they taken from Rebekah with no questions asked? Are the accepted moral judgments simply 'there', among the social facts like pieces of lumber to be used by Christian love in constructing a proper human dwelling place. That would be rule-agapism of the 'social engineering' type. Or is law and a socially accepted ethic the product of a multitude of past acts of obedience among the children of God (*rule*-agapism), and in this sense to be received from our elder brother into dialogue

---

[1] *Christian Morals Today*, p. 10.
[2] ibid., p. 20.   [3] ibid., p. 34.

23

with contemporary Christian conscience? This would mean that the Christian life in all ages consists of an unceasing dialogue and tension between rule-agapism and act-agapism. Or is a conventionally accepted ethic, the net which love needs, the product of an even older brother, the *jus gentium*, in which are contained principles of perhaps general validity, perhaps less than general validity? That would be a form of mixed agapism in which elements of the other way in are obtained from an Esau whose goods and prowess do not themselves belong to or originate with the people of God. Robinson addresses himself to none of these questions, except that we may suppose he would suspect that the last possibility must be based on a belief in 'occult' realities.

This is the place to append the fundamental objection to be brought against this author's Christian ethical analysis, and it is an objection that is even more telling against the unexamined assumptions of other Christian situationalists today. These lectures discuss three of the polarities in Christian ethics under the headings, 'Fixity and Freedom', 'Law and Love', and 'Authority and Experience'. Bishop Robinson asserts that these are 'really ... the *same* polarity under three *aspects*'.[1] This has to be questioned and rejected at the beginning of any discussion of Christian ethics today. This asserts that 'fixity', 'law' and 'authority' are but aspects of or alternative ways of expressing one way in; while 'freedom', 'love' and 'experience' belong together in forming the other pole. Robinson has his conclusion from the start and begs the most essential question when he identifies the antinomy of Law and Gospel (Love) with those other antinomies. This leads him metaphorically to identify law with 'the rocks' and the Gospel (Love) with 'the rapids'.[2] It is, of course, the method of act-agapism that is enshrined in the view that these chapter titles do but state the same polarity under slightly differing aspects; and we have seen that Bishop Robinson is not consistently concerned with rapidly changing acts of love. I had heard that the Gospel was rather a Rock, and in no case should one thoughtlessly presume that Love may not lead to constancy (rule-agapism).[3] It is a

---

[1] ibid., p. 11 (italics added).   [2] ibid., pp. 18, 20.

[3] For this reason, I am pleased to observe that the quotations Bishop Robinson takes from my *Basic Christian Ethics* (Scribner's, 1950) are all used in his chapter on 'Law and Love', none when he is dealing with 'Fixity and Freedom' or with 'Authority and Experience'. From my youth up I have known that the dialectic

common and basic error of Christian situationalism to begin with the premise that *agapé* in its freedom cannot bind itself unreservedly and change not.

2. *Working Rules*

Taking Bishop Robinson's 'way in' upon moral and social questions, there may be two sorts of rules which are the product of love as it shapes itself for action. These will be discussed in this and the next numbered paragraph. The first is that there are provisional, 'working rules', of less than general validity in which love finds expression, but which love in its sovereign freedom remains ready to change at any moment by adopting another rule, or by making an exception in a particular situation while leaving the rule still standing as ordinarily wise and required by love.

Out there, there is only 'a world of relativities' into which a Christian enters with his single absolute (*agapé*). With these relativities he makes contact and in their midst he serves his neighbour 'through a casuistry obedient to love'.[1] So far, this is act-agapism working over or through the pieces of lumber of which experience consists. So far, love does not itself have the breadth or substance to be productive of rules, habits, styles, 'working' or otherwise; nor does love itself seem to be the agent that substantially builds up 'the bank of experience' or edifies the materials of experience into some more acceptable order. There is in *Honest to God* mainly the assertion *that* a social order will be needed and confidence that it will be *there*. If the Christian shores this up or keeps it in repair, it will be not from principles of his own which lead rather to *agapé*-acts that come from and penetrate to the person; or it will be simply because some social fabric is necessary. Thus, the *agapé*-situationalism that is mainly characteristic of the chapter on ethics in *Honest to God* is *ethically* quite unqualified.

The possibility of securing the minimum moral foundations of a social ethics (if these do not devolve from love itself) by recognising some God-given structures amid the relationships into which we are called is likewise passed over. This can be

of Law and Gospel is by no means the same dialectic as that which goes on between fixity and freedom and between authority and experience. Does not Love teach with an authority that neither results from experience nor relies upon it, or upon an 'inductive method'? And does not Love exhibit itself in constancies that a less worthy freedom sometimes falsely calls fixities?

[1] *Honest to God*, p. 116, q. Joseph Fletcher, op. cit., p. 10.

seen in what is said about the prismatic case (of response to the needs and claims of more than one neighbour) in which the inner logic must be discovered by which there evolves a Christian social ethic out of the teachings of Jesus. Jesus does not adjudicate conflicting claims. Nevertheless the disciple of Christ will have to ask himself 'who is going to maintain the widow after she has pledged her total means of support or the children of the man who has given everything to a beggar'. Of course, love must consider these and a multitude of other different needs and claims; and it will consider them all 'equally unreservedly'. One may ask, Does love not *devolve* or *discern* amid these relationships some ethically important differences between near and distant neighbours, or any reason to approve the special care of one's own children? To such questions, Robinson gives no definitive answer, but only a situational decision in the presence, it would seem, of equal, myriad, chaotic claims. '. . . If we have the heart of the matter in us, if our eye is single, then love will find the way, its own particular way in every individual situation.'[1] This seems to reject rule-agapism since it implies that love is *productive* of acts only and never also of rules for the ordering of human reality; and it also rejects agapism mixed with some other source of the guidance of action since it implies that love *finds* only decisions to be made and acts to be done, never any order or at least no moral order *in* the world of surrounding personal claims.

Robinson's viewpoint is different or more fully expounded in *Christian Morals Today*. Here there are two alternatives each of which goes beyond pure situationalism: there are working rules of less than general validity or there are rules of general validity which embody love. Either or both of these views may be the implication of the basic normative propostion of agapism, that '*nothing else* makes a thing right or wrong'.[2]

There is not much to be said about the first type of rules—working rules of less than general validity—except to say that from age to age love is the architect of them. The 'church of the old covenant helped to provide a series of [moral nets] for the societies in which it lived, *refining it successively* . . .'. So also

[1] ibid., p. 112.

[2] ibid., p. 119. It is a rather hopeless task, however, to convince Christian people that the religious reiteration of this premise is no substitute for ethical reflection; or to convince Christian ethicists today that this premise of general ethics does not of itself lead to one conclusion only: act-agapism.

there are 'blocs of ethical material' in the New Testment which are a fabric for the upbuilding of the person and the community. But what comes to us of unconditional importance through the teachings of the church 'also *judges* that net, and enables us to recognise that what may be the embodiment of the divine command in one generation can be its distortion in the next'.[1] Christians are bound to construct a net, to repair the net, but also to criticise[2] and transform it in the direction that love requires. 'The plea for the priority of love fully recognises the obligation upon Christians in each generation to help fashion and frame the moral net which will best preserve the body and soul of their *society*.'[3] This is one form of rule-agapism.

3. *General Rules*

However, there are also generally valid rules of action that love itself implies. Bishop Robinson states the thesis of pure rule-agapism when he writes, 'In Christian ethics the only pure statement is the command to love: every other injunction depends on it and is an explication or application of it.' For there *are* other injunctions, e.g. the proscription of cruelty to children or rape. These derivative rules are sufficient to show that 'there are some things of which one can say that it is so inconceivable that they could ever be an expression of love . . . that they are for Christians always wrong.'[4] Such moral injunctions are simple corollaries or implications of covenant-love. They are as unconditionally wrong as love is unconditionally right.

This statement that there are some things that are 'always wrong' seems to contradict the statement in Robinson's earlier book that 'nothing can of itself always be labelled as "wrong"'.[5] He therefore explains that 'they are so persistently wrong *for that reason*', i.e. for the reason that it is inconceivable that they could ever be an expression of love.[6] Let us try to imagine a set of conditions that might be said to justify an exception to one of these rules. Suppose that the only survivors of a nuclear holocaust are the Bishop of Woolwich and a sex-frustrated

---

[1] *Christian Morals Today*, p. 17 (italics added).
[2] ibid., p. 18.   [3] ibid., p. 31.
[4] *Christian Morals Today*, p. 16.   [5] *Honest to God*, p. 118.
[6] *Christian Morals Today*, p. 16. The quotations that follow are from this same page.

female missionary of child-bearing age. Would rape be justified in order to replenish the earth? This would be as certainly wrong in an ethic such as Robinson holds which prohibits the use of a person as a mere, unwilling means for any ulterior purpose, as it would be judged wrong in an ethic that derives its Christian substance from the supernatural end of man and refuses to allow this to be replaced by the supreme good of the continuation of persons like us upon this planet. Therefore, it is quite clear that Robinson should not have immediately translated (as he seems to do) the notation 'always wrong' into '*working rules* which for *practical purposes* one can lay down as guides to Christian conduct'. An extrinsic explanation would have to be given for this strange reluctance to let *agapé* reach certitude.

Robinson immediately rises again to the procedure of pure rule-agapism when he writes that 'these various commandments are comprehended under the one command of love and based on it. Apart from this there are no unbreakable rules.' If one wanted to express the whole task of Christian ethical reflection, that last statement should read: in and from love, there *are* or there may be unbreakable rules, and the question to be relentlessly pressed is what these rules are.

The fact that there are some things that are 'always wrong for the reason that it is inconceivable that they could ever be an expression of love' does not remove the fact that these things are *inherently* wrong, wrong in themselves, even though this is because of the lovelessness that is always in them. To say otherwise would be rather like a rule-utilitarian who felt bound always to be singing the praises of the principle of utility, and who as a consequence refuses ever to talk about rules of action except to explain that anything that is wrong is wrong for the reason that it is inconceivable that under any circumstances it could be an expression of utility. Such a man would simply not be getting on with the business of doing utilitarian ethics.

It is always necessary to begin somewhere—even if it is with rape or promiscuity or prostitution—in order to discover whether there are any rules of conduct embodying love, or acts only. But there is more extensive elaboration of rule-agapism in Robinson's book on ethics. He began his first lecture by saying that he might not have delivered any of these lectures but for 'a strong sense that *keeping promises* is a rather important

28

part of Christian ethics'.[1] Moreover, in answer to the accusation that the chapter on 'the new morality' in *Honest to God* could be used to give warrant to Mr Profumo's *act* of lying to the House of Commons in order to save his family from public disgrace, Bishop Robinson writes finely of 'the searching claims of Christian love. Such love demands that we lay ourselves open. . . . To "save" a person one loves from the opportunities of making this response could not be described in Christian terms as "necessary for the sake of love".' This seems to introduce the requirement of *truth telling*; and, indeed, so far is Robinson's understanding of Christian love from being a mere sentiment that it would be surprising if the searching claims of Christian love were productive of anything short of these and other rules of conduct. And later on he writes that 'I would, of course, be the first to agree that there are a whole class of actions—like stealing, lying, killing, committing adultery—which are so fundamentally destructive of human relationships that no differences of century or society can change their character'.[2] These are all promising suggestions for an exploration that has in view answering the question whether *agapé* is productive of rules also or of acts only.

However, Robinson promptly drew back again from his own best thoughts. 'But this does not, of course, mean', he wrote, 'that stealing and lying can in certain circumstances never be right.' To support this he said something that is entirely mistaken: 'All Christians would admit that they could be.' Never have Christians—at least not those Christians whose vocation it is to reflect as ethicists upon the nature of the Christian life—admitted any such thing. Instead they have asked: what is the meaning of the forbidden theft, what is the meaning of truth-telling, what is the forbidden murder? They have explored or deepened or restricted the moral meaning of these categories or rules of conduct. There was once a man who was asked to define the difference between adultery and fornication; and who, hesitating a moment, replied: 'Well, I've tried them both, and to me there wasn't any difference.' To which the proper reply is that the question did not ask him to take the 'inductive approach'; and his answer makes it clear that he is greatly in need of clarifying his categories.

[1] ibid., pp. 7-8 (italics added).
[2] ibid., p. 16, from which subsequent quotations are also taken.

The work of Christian ethics in clarifying the categories—truth-telling, promise-keeping, theft, lying, murder—is not ordinarily a matter of love allowing an exception to a fixed definition of these terms but a matter of love illuminating the meaning of them. What looks like a right to deviate from the rule is really love's duty to do so because of the love-full meaning of the 'natural justice' summarised in these classes of actions or because of an expansion or deepening of the meaning of these rules of conduct. This is the way love sensitises and instructs conscience.

An illustration of this is the traditional treatment of 'justified theft'. This was an 'exception' only when externally or statistically viewed. The moral reasoning on which this piece of casuistry was based was a love-informed determination of the created destination of property right to the common good or common use. This was 'love's casuistry', and then with the principles governing property in mind love proceeded to the ordering of human reality generally and to particular cases of application. It was the bourgeois period with its notions of absolute property right that made the prohibition of theft not only a fixed rule but a fixed rule with a certain and a non-Christian moral meaning so that thereafter theft could only be a (forbidden) exception.

Robinson's ethic of the exceptional case is a product of the control bourgeois ethics still has over his ethical categories. We shall see that to great degree a bourgeois understanding of 'the marriage line' or a Victorian stress on social respectability and legality are also determinative of the 'old morality' he wishes to overcome. This leads him in the direction of a possibly responsible exception to *this* rule, rather than always to deeper reflection about the Christian meaning of marriage. Robinson's ethic of the exception was more unqualified in *Honest to God*, there where he is trying to show that 'nothing can of itself always be labelled as "wrong"'; and where he illustrates this mathematically by saying that 'sex relations before marriage' and 'divorce' may be wrong 'in 99 cases or even 100 cases out of 100, but they are not intrinsically so, for the only intrinsic evil is lack of love'.[1]

---

[1] *Honest to God*, p. 118. Here again the author's doing of 'special ethics' is inhibited because he simply keeps on reiterating his 'general ethics', or his systematic justification of any rules or acts.

In the next section we will be dealing with a Christian ethicist —Paul Lehmann—who, in contrast to Robinson's most extreme statements of act-agapism, has set himself the task of expounding a situational ethic that specialises in the exception —or, if that were possible, makes a general principle of it.

We have seen now the extensive development of rule-agapism in Robinson's recent book. There is more. There where he is stressing the fact that the *content* of Christian morals seems to change from age to age, he points out that an unconditional, unvarying love in a multitude of responses 'produces in Christians, however different or diversely placed, a direction, a cast, a style of life, which is recognisably and gloriously the same'.[1] Before coming to '*what* precisely' Christians must do, the 'direction', 'cast' and 'style of life' which is recognisably and gloriously the same would seem to be worth attention and further explication. This might have to be in quasi-aesthetic terms, or in imagery more than in concepts. Still that would be an important part of the way to do Christian ethics. It would be in some measure an explication of 'love's casuistry'. Of course, the Holy Spirit doubtless puts it into the mouth of a radical Christian responsiveness what that direction or cast or style shall be, if after the fact these acts turn out to be *recognisably* and gloriously the same. But if there is any work for Christian ethics to do, if there is any virtue in systematic reflection upon the nature of the Christian life, then that style of life will be its subject matter. In any case, a Christian ethics which contains this one statement alone—*that* Christian responses have a recognisably common style—no longer belongs to the class of act-agapism; and it ought no longer to demand unconditional surrender of the view that there are qualities that have general validity in Christian ethics which arise from love itself, and not acts only.

Finally, we need to take up the question of what Bishop Robinson deliberately calls 'the *limits* of pre-marital sex for engaged couples'.[2] That possibility was mathematically instanced in *Honest to God*; and we have already surrounded the exception the author means to talk about by ruling out prostitution, promiscuity, and adultery as always wrong because it is so inconceivable that these things could ever be an expression

---

[1] *Christian Morals Today*, p. 13.
[2] ibid., p. 32, from which page subsequent quotations are also taken.

of love.[1] The question now to be raised is whether in trying to surround the exception more closely and thus get a grip on it (under the heading of 'the *limits* of pre-marital sex for engaged couples'), it has not disappeared altogether. If this is so, then the question is whether *honesty* in sexual *ethics* does not require the Christian moralist to say so, and to state the rule that *truthfully expresses* the personal commitment he knows to be required in sexually responsible relations.

These are the issues which arise in connexion with what might be called the problem of 'justified fornication'—if the reader will know that I am able to discuss cases and classes of things calmly and intend no prejudice by using this expression. To speak of 'the limits of pre-marital sex for engaged couples' already marks off a class of things within the genus of things formerly called fornication (which itself is clearly distinguishable from both adultery and promiscuity); and it raises the question about the possible justification of this more restricted class of actions. The really remarkable thing is that when Bishop Robinson directs his Christian reflection to 'the *limits* of pre-marital sex for engaged couples' he can actually find no responsible case of it within these limits, and that what he says in general allows for none. This will be my final example from his writings of the edification to be found in the thought that there may be rules of action that best embody love.

Having introduced this question, Robinson says at once: 'I believe the nexus between bed and board, between sex and the sharing of life at every level, must be pressed as strongly as ever by those who really care for persons as persons'. This goes quite a long way on the basis of his 'way in' upon moral problems. This is called, however, a 'working rule'. From the context at this point it is not clear whether by 'working rule' he means a rule that is somewhat less than generally valid and to which there still may be an exception (yet one now very narrowly surrounded in view of the pattern of responsibility

---

[1] These rules of conduct are much clearer in the Bishop's writings than they are in the moral revolution he is so anxious to take for granted in the doing of Christian ethics. That ancient profession has today been brought to ruin and disrepute by amateur competition. The age of chivalry is not dead in that its code and travelling minstrels can praise adultery no less than sex before marriage as a precious expression of freedom-in-love. And while promiscuity is not ruled in, it is also not ruled out by the new morality, except that persons in love should not concentrate on it, and except for the law of nature which makes it quite impossible for a man to have sexual relations with two women at the same time.

this rule affords); or whether this expression only means a *derivative* rule, a rule that depends on but definitely follows from 'what a deep concern for persons as whole persons, in their entire social context, really requires'.[1] If the latter is the case, then we may have discovered another class of things that are always wrong because it is so inconceivable that they could ever be an expression of love when it is strong and true and wholly honest.

This conclusion becomes clear on another page, to which Bishop Robinson is driven by his sense that *agapé* is the most 'searching and demanding criterion of ethical judgement'.[2] Persons who, deeply in love, are asking themselves about the limits of their pre-marital sexual relations should ask 'what deep Christian love for the other person as a whole person (as opposed to exploitation and enjoyment, even if it is mutual) really demands—and that within the total social context'. Unfortunately the answer that is suggested to this question is confused by what I have called a bourgeois conception of 'the marriage line'; and the Bishop's quite correct judgment that acts within *this* line (of legal marriage) may not be based on a loving and caring and responsible relationship and that acts outside *this* line need not be not so. But he writes boldly and without qualification: 'Outside marriage sex is *bound* to be the expression of less than an unreserved sharing and commitment of one person to another.'[3] Now, unless I fail to grasp some mysterious difference between a 'bound' and a 'line', Robinson has drawn a correct boundary, beneath and replacing in principle the merely legal line he began with, but a boundary none the less. This rule is said to be general, and unexceptional. It is in fact what Christianity has always meant by marriage, or the responsible consent to one another that alone makes marriage. In this sense there is nothing pre-marital about what Robinson is talking about. Beginning by asking about the limits upon pre-marital sexual relations between engaged couples, it turns out that marriage covers the whole ground of the action sought to be justified; and there remain only legal or practical considerations about whether public acknowledgment can or should be secured for the fact that a mutual acknowledgment of marital responsibility and the marriage relation itself has been assumed by the partners.

[1] ibid., p. 33.   [2] ibid., p. 42.   [3] ibid., p. 42 (italics added).

Enough has been said, I suppose, for the reader to be able to frame a reply to Robinson's rhetorical question: 'Do we really want the furtiveness taken out of pre-marital sex?'[1] However, it is in order to remark upon the ethics of non-furtiveness (since the purpose of this essay is to delineate rule-agapism as among the possible methods and systems of Christian ethics, and not to give a complete account of Christian sex and marriage ethics). The remark is simply this: a rule proscribing furtiveness as undesirable and honesty as desirable says a great deal about the Christian style of life; and if only this were known to be what love requires, anyone who had any concern with strengthening the *ethos* and an accepted ethic in this regard could not then avoid the consequence that the better society becomes the more furtiveness would have to be practised furtively and lack of truthfulness would have to be dissimulated.

I draw a line here in order not to associate together the views of Robinson and H. A. Williams, who is a rather clear if un-developed case of act-agapism in Christian ethical analysis. Eric Mascall's chapter on 'Pumping out the Bilge'[2] is a clever and correct answer to Williams' essay in *Soundings*; but I rather think his error needs to be more carefully identified. Also, it is Williams and not Robinson who deserves the attribution by the Archbishop of Canterbury of the belief that 'fornication may be right if it is thought to produce good'.[3]

Williams begins with an unexceptional statement of Christian normative ethics: 'generous self-giving love is the ultimate moral value'.[4] This leads him at once to an ethics of the exception from those classes of things, such as theft, once described as wicked in themselves and on which we have already commented sufficiently in the foregoing. Then we come to sexual ethics. On this subject there has been 'an enormous amount of double-think', which Williams replaces by a similar degree of single-case thinking. He takes up the now famous case of the prostitute in the Greek film *Never on Sunday*. She picks up a young sailor, who, however, is in deep distress over

---

[1] ibid., p. 44. The answer, in part: any society, I suppose, needs to leave room for *secret* marriages, and perhaps for common law marriage subsequently placing the enforcement of the law behind a responsibility that was entailed.

[2] *Up and Down in Adria*. London: The Faith Press, 1963, ch. 2. See also *Four Anchors from the Stern*, ed. by Alan Richardson, London: S.C.M. Press, pp. 32-34.

[3] Michael Ramsey: *Image Old and New*. London: S.P.C.K., 1963, p. 13.

[4] *Soundings* (ed. by A. R. Vidler). Cambridge: University Press, 1962, p. 80.

34

his capacity to perform an act of sexual intercourse. 'The prostitute gives herself to him in such a way that he acquires confidence and self-respect. He goes away a deeper fuller person than he came in.' This, Williams writes, is 'an act of charity which proclaims the glory of God. The man is now equipped as he was not before.'[1] And upon the not unlike case in the English film, *The Mark*, of a man who was unable to desire sexually a mature woman of his own age, Williams' comment is: 'Will he be able to summon up the necessary courage or not? When he does, and they sleep together, he has been made whole. And where there is healing, there is Christ, whatever the Church may say about fornication. And the appropriate response is—Glory to God in the Highest.'[2]

Now, I suppose that a radically monotheistic faith such as that of Christianity will find a way of interpreting *theologically* all that is and all the actions there are in the world; and that it will refuse to place anything outside of God's world in a dualistic realm of wickedness. Under the first article of the creed, we say that where there is any being or measure or order or beauty, there God is. He enables the power of the murderer with his knife. And under the second article of the creed, if we take this with the seriousness of a Karl Barth, we know that covenant is the inner basis of the whole creation and that all the prostitutes and bankers who ever lived now have their beings and the reality of their lives in Him. We should, therefore, not be surprised to find more or less dim or more or less clear traces of agapistic attitudes and actions to be characteristic of this our common humanity (just as a less Christocentric anthropology would find among all men a potentiality, e.g. for natural justice).

A Christian, therefore, might not find this an altogether incredible portrait of a prostitute, where another sort of man who takes an inductive approach might note that she was a fictional character, and that prostitutes are really not like that in real life. Even a resolutely Christocentric interpretation of the being and nature of acts of prostitution will find it possible to give greater credence to the evidence that a prostitute who plies her trade while genuinely giving herself in sexual love to one man must precisely not allow herself to be self-giving in sexual

[1] ibid., p. 81.
[2] ibid., p. 82.

35

relations with all the others. One might find in this a clearer trace of the fact that covenant is the inner reality and the goal of sexual creation and of man-womanhood in all its breadth and depth; and conclude from this that man-womanhood was not made for such casual acts even if it may happen that healing takes place and one comes away a deeper, fuller person than he went in. He might, of course, exclaim: Glory to the God of all covenants! He might return thanks for the fact that he had encountered *in act* more of a woman-person than he was a man-person. But it would still be the case that another person bore him in covenant and took his injury upon herself more than he bore her flesh or cared for her in the covenant of life with life. He should know this; or if he does not there is a deeper fault in him than any anxiety about his sexual powers and one less easily taken away. If he does know this, he might then *begin* to do Christian ethics.

More important it is to call attention to the fact—for which, of course, Williams is not responsible—that in our meagre times the literary portrait of the saintly prostitute has become a matter of act saintliness (and we can't even be sure of that, since it is the *effects*, the works, and not the *being* of sainthood that is in evidence). In Dostoievsky's Christ-figure, Sonia, it is her suffering and not her self-giving which her prostitution sym-bolises, while her healing love is embodied in her relations with the miserable little family she sustains by her earnings, in the inner integrity of her whole personal style of life, and in relation to Raskolnikov's forgiveness and his possible resurrection from the dead. It is also a profound insight of Dostoievsky's that, when a woman is sought out of great or weak sexual need on the part of a man who wants only to use her, his sexual desire itself collapses if, she consenting, he catches a glimpse of the mystery of her personal freedom that his penetration is not going to touch or succeed in violating or she bestow in thus physically yielding. This, too, is more than a trace of the fact that human sexuality is creation toward covenant; and, by comparison with Williams' illustrations drawn from contem-porary literature, we can see how far from Christian ground the present age has proceeded in its concern for the *individual* psyche.

This should enable us now to put our fingers on the formative idea and the essential clue to an understanding of act-agapism in its present vogue. The language of it is still Christian. Much is made of spiritual freedom, of love, and of freedom-in-love. But for all that, the basic philosophy of act-agapism is drawn from no Christian source. It is drawn rather from the atomistic individualism of secular thought in the modern period. This continues to be the acid that eats away at moral relations, and at the very idea that there are moral bonds between man and man or between one moment and another.

The model for this freedom-in-love and an ethic of atomistic acts in Christian clothing is actually Jean Jacques Rousseau (making allowance for a liberal addition of Freudianism). For Rousseau there can be no bond (but only bargains) between two contracting individuals because there can and should be no bond established between one atomistic moment of willing or consenting and the next, and the next after that, which does not too much bind the latter and derogate upon the freedom of these later moments of willing. The sovereign individual may indeed say, 'I now will actually what this other person wills, or at least what he says he wills'. Is not this the basic premise of modern 'contract' marriage which has invaded even the mind of the church today? But the sovereign individual cannot say without loss of freedom-in-act: 'What he wills tomorrow [or what, e.g. marriage requires tomorrow], I too shall will.'[1] The biblical covenant view of marriage, which lies behind our marriage law, affirms the will's competence to bind itself from one moment to another throughout all change, and therefore its competence to bind itself to another and thus to exhibit a fuller freedom.

It is of the very greatest importance that we understand the connexion between the presence or absence of bonds or structures between man and man and the presence or absence of bonds or structures relating one moment to another. If act-agapism fails to discover any moral bonds between man and man, this is because it can find no sustaining moral bond between the present moment of action and a later moment of action. If rule-agapism devolves or discerns such bonds, this will be because on its view love connects one moment of action with another (pure rule-agapism), or finds that they are in fact already morally joined together (mixed rule-agapism).

I must add that for Mr Williams' view of Christ's healing presence it would seem that the name of that film should not

---

[1] *The Social Contract*, Bk. II, ch. I.

have been *Never on Sunday* but *Always on Sunday* since that is the day the sacrament is enacted. The prostitute gave that man an outward and visible and moreover an effective sign of an inner and invisible work of the grace that seems most important for act-agapism (individual wholeness, or even just act-wholeness). This was at least a sacramental, or a signal instance not of course of an ordinance but of an action in which freedom-in-love came to concentration in material things.

For this same reason it may be observed that in some quarters divorce would seem to be a more appropriate sacrament than marriage. Marriage, traditionally and rightly understood, is something to which two people belong, in which they belong to one another and which belongs to neither of the parties. It is a rule of life and a moral bond. It is a cause between them and greater than they are or than any of the acts of love in marriage. Of course, according to pure act-agapism, there is such a thing as marriage and perhaps it is deserving of that name. But marriage on this view consists of its renewal every moment in which the parties say, I now will what this person wills as from the depths of personhood we meet one another with a love that remains as free as before. It will be tragic, of course, if this marriage comes to an end; and we would not have set out along the conventional route society provides if we had such an ending in mind. Still the freedom of divorce is a material moment that exhibits in outward and visible signs the freedom-in-loving-acts of which the marriage all along consisted. It is the clearest prismatic way to make manifest the whole meaning of marriage. Thus, divorce that manifests freedom would seem a more appropriate sacrament than that moment from which we set out together by words and acts that seemed to say, What this person wills tomorrow or what our marriage requires tomorrow I too shall will and her I will cherish through all change. The moment of freedom in divorce as the sacrament would seem to be the logical conclusion in an age that gives paramount position to Rousseau's un-binding love, which today is even powerfully affecting our understanding of Christian freedom. Such is definitely not the conclusion to be drawn whenever and wherever the freedom of God's love in binding Himself to the world is taken as the model for all the covenants among men.[1]

[1] The above does not necessarily establish the conclusion that marriage is quite

I read recently an article on American family law that can serve as a test case or 'thought-experiment' that may help to determine whether it is individualistic freedom-in-love or the requirements of a responsible love that is at work in contemporary culture. This may also serve to make clear on which side of this line are to be located the operative principles of those of us doing Christian ethics today. For a comparatively short time, Anglo-American law has experimented with the freedom of divorce, this having been introduced into the century-old tradition of western morals less than a hundred years ago. It would not be surprising if there are vested rights and real needs of some of the parties involved in a divorce decree that our modern law of marriage and divorce has not yet learned how to protect in the situation created by remarriage following divorce. Has the law done all it should have done to protect the rights of the 10 million children of the total of 4 million American marriages that ended in divorce from 1944-54?

The legal article[1] to which I refer affirms that 'the basic assumption (and fundamental contradiction) of family law in America has been that a father can give substantially equal opportunities to the children of his first marriage while simultaneously extending equal benefits to the offspring of his second (or third) marriage. To state the assumption is to reveal the basic problems it conceals.' Granted that the writ of the law cannot insure all of the personal values that are theirs to the children of broken marriages, should we continue to allow their support, future education, etc., to be made a matter over which their parents *bargain*? 'The results of giving to ex-husbands the privilege of having two sets of children have become alarmingly clear. The allocations of public money for aid to dependent children rise each year. . . .' Therefore, this author concludes, 'some more legally satisfactory way must be devised and adopted by which society can act in a responsible and just manner towards the millions of American children whose rights to economic security and equality cannot be said to be

indissoluble, but only that today most proponents and very many Christian proponents of its dissolubility base this on a theology of the individual that is entirely non-Christian even when this sounds highly Christian in its stress on the person and on 'freedom'.

[1] Robert F. Drinan, S. J.: *The Rights of Children Whose Parents Are Divorced.* University of Illinois *Law Forum*, Family Law, Vol. 1962, Winter, pp. 618-32.

treated with elementary due process in the ordinary divorce proceedings'.

In addition to a humorous reference to a system of 'divorce-insurance', this author seriously proposes that a separate lawyer be appointed to represent the children in divorce proceeding and afterward for the years of their nonage. Thus would society stand *in loco parentis* for the parents who failed them in order to insure that the minimum rights of the children are not infringed by any subsequent remarriage with its new quiverful of children. This would mean that there might be divorce decrees specifically stipulating that the divorced parents cannot remarry where this would clearly make it impossible for them to fulfil their responsibilities toward already existing children. In any case, divorced parents would have to assume the burden of proving that they can adequately support two sets of children before they would be legally permitted to remarry.

Now, I am at the moment not interested in considering all of the arguments for or against this proposal for the reform of family law. It may be that its total effects would be to cause worse to befall. Still I think that this affords us an interesting test case for determining in thought whether freedom-in-love or a responsible love is the basic premise in our thinking about moral problems. According as our initial reactions to this suggestion vary, the secrets of many a heart will be revealed, and perhaps we can see from this whether we are primarily interested in an ethics of venereal freedom or an ethics of venereal responsibilities. I do not say that this proves the case for rule-agapism as against act-agapism. But I do say that this experiment in thought discloses what in many instances act-agapism comes down to. It is the boundless freedom of atomistic individualism that hides behind the terminology of Christian ethics as this is often used today. By this disclosure, the possibility of act-agapism has not been ruled out. However, the meaning of *agapé* should be kept quite clear. *Agapé* means, as Bishop Robinson said, 'the overriding, unconditional claim of God's utterly gracious yet utterly demanding rule of righteous love'.[1] While such an ethical standard may still allow room for act-agapism, we nevertheless have seen how it contains an inward pressure toward rule-agapism as also necessary in any adequate elaboration of Christian ethics.

[1] *Christian Morals Today*, p. 12.

IV

THE CONTEXTUALISM OF PAUL LEHMANN

WE have a more formidable position to place under scrutiny in the ethics that is being done by Professor Paul Lehmann of Union Theological Seminary in New York. Unlike John A. T. Robinson, Paul Lehmann makes the exception the rule. It will be seen that he is a thoroughgoing proponent of act-agapism, in the broad sense in which I am using this term of Frankena's. I would call his an act-*koinonia* ethics. At the same time, Lehmann gives extended exposition of the asserted *theological* basis for a Christian situationalism in ethics. This will enable us to abandon for the moment Frankena's classification of possible normative Christian ethical theories, in order to take up the problem of methods in Christian ethics from the point of view of its foundation in Christian theology. What does Christian theology imply for the doing of Christian ethics, for the methods of ethics and the meaning of the Christian life?

Paul Lehmann's book[1] is about *the context*—the theological and ecclesiological context—of Christian ethics. Despite the title, it is only quite subordinately a book about the meaning of ethics in this context. A second volume is promised that, presumably, will elaborate the author's views on substantive ethics. This should also undertake to demonstrate 'the contextual character of Christian ethics', to which only one chapter is devoted in the present volume. To that chapter the present essay will direct the reader's attention in the end. For here must be found the practical demonstrations that contextual Christian ethics succeeds (as Lehmann asserts it does) in overcoming the gap between the ethical claim and the ethical act; whether, if so, it then succeeds in avoiding on the one hand the supposed irrelevance and impotence of a preceptual understanding of Christian norms and on the other the capriciousness of ethical relativism; and finally whether it is a virtue in ethical reflection to have done all this.

[1] *Ethics in a Christian Context.* New York and Evanston, Harper and Row, Publishers, 1963. 367 pages. $5.00.

The author knows, and it is to be hoped that the readers of this review-article will know, that the highest respect to be paid a book which is the result of years of serious study and reflection is to wrestle with it all night long even at the risk of getting oneself wounded in the thigh. Besides, someone needs to challenge the easy assumption that is formative of church pronouncements precisely today when a Christian context has ceased to be formative of human life—to the effect that 'the ethic which gives point and direction to the witness of the church to its risen Lord is eschatological ... trinitarian ... contextual'.[1] The sudden introduction of that final, non-biblical, non-theological word should be disturbing to anyone concerned with Christian ethics. It forms no ethical trinity with the other two biblical categories; yet it is used today as if it did.

After three centuries in which every revival of Protestant Christianity has revived less of it, and after the recent decades of an increasingly Christ-less religiousness in the churches, it was predictable that celebrated theologians would begin their futile search for a religion-less Christianity to proclaim in a secular world that is supposed to have 'come of age'. Lehmann may yield too much to this Bonhoefferish mood. Yet the announced intention of this book is to show that 'there are insights and conceptions rooted in the faith and ethics of the Reformation which are possessed of *formative power* for ethical theory and practice today'.[2] The question is whether, in order for Christian insights to be formative of human life, we do not have to know more 'about what God is doing in the world' than 'what we read in the Bible' and 'in the papers'.[3] In any case, we may be able to learn from Lehmann whether a full-bodied understanding of the Christian life can be recovered, or even articulated, simply by dwelling upon the immediate encounter of today's world with the *theological ultimates* ingredient to the Christian context, without a significant Christian *ethical analysis* and guidance fully elaborated in between.

---

[1] *Relations between Church and State in the United States of America*, adopted by the 175th General Assembly of the United Presbyterian Church in the United States of America, May 1963. Office of the General Assembly, Witherspoon Building, Philadelphia, Pa.

[2] p. 13 (italics added).

[3] p. 74.

A

The Context of Christian Ethics

The author says many things about the context of Christian ethics that are both true and important. Moreover, he knows that primacy must be given to this context in all Christian action and reflection about morality. 'This is why', he correctly says, 'it makes all the difference in the world . . . in what context your ethical insights and practices are nourished.'[1] Still the soil is not the same as the tree, nor are its roots the branches; nor, even, the composition of the nourishment the same as the fruit expected.

Christian behaviour roots in God's action as this has been and is made known to us. Several statements can, therefore, be made ostensibly or only partly about ethics in a Christian context but chiefly and correctly about the context of Christian ethics. Each of these propositions points to some ingredient in the soil that nourishes the Christian life, and which Christian ethics must take as its point of departure. These are, broadly speaking, *theological* statements which summarise Lehmann's understanding of the basis and the environs of Christian ethics: (1) Christian ethics is the ethics of the *koinonia*. (2) It calls for obedience to what God is doing in the world. (3) It means response to what God is doing to keep human life *human*. (4) It is Christological or the ethics of messianism.[2]

---

[1] p. 65.

[2] These four summary statements could be preceded by another in the first place, making five propositions in all. I would formulate this affirmatively as: 'Christian ethics is theological ethics', with a view to embracing in this statement the fanfare about *hermeneutics* with which the book opens. Although Lehmann says that Christian ethics is a 'theological discipline', he most often expresses this negatively: Christian ethics is *not* biblical or New Testament ethics. Or else he expresses the same point in an as yet empty statement *that* there is a hermeneutical problem. The fact is that, just as epistemology (or man's ways of knowing) is by itself an empty science or one that can be best pursued in connexion with ontology or in the course of debate about the modes of being, so the principles of hermeneutics or the science of interpretation can best be exhibited in the course of actually interpreting Scripture and in debates about its theological meaning. This is indeed the way Lehmann proceeds to use Scripture on many, many pages of this volume. Despite his opening gambit about there being a hermeneutical problem, and Christian ethics as a theological discipline that is not the same as biblical ethics, he nowhere tells us what are his hermeneutical principles or argues for them unless he does this by using them throughout the whole of the volume in the actual interpretations of Scripture he proposes. This seems to me to be an altogether correct procedure, and the only fruitful one. But then he ought not to have reduced to a footnote (pp. 26-27) two rather good books in the field of Christian ethics that likewise proceed at once to the interpretation of Scripture (without, however, an initial and purely ceremonial bow in the direction of hermeneutical

43

We shall first examine what Lehmann says under each of these summary theological, ecclesiological and Christological statements. In every case Lehmann must be criticised for having an inadequate understanding of the basis and the environs of the Christian life; and it will be pointed out that this leads him to a prejudice in favour of what he calls a contextual Christian ethics and what I call act-*koinonia* ethics. Then we will be prepared to take up his version of contextual ethics directly, and what he says about the particular moral problems he chooses to discuss. In the end, there is need for drastic revision of both Lehmann's theological statements and his constructive statements about Christian ethics; and the one weakness is a function of the other.

1. *Koinonia ethics*

Christian behaviour roots in the *koinonia*. Christian ethics is *koinonia* ethics. It is 'reflection upon the question, and its answer: What am I as a believer in Jesus Christ and a member of His church, to do?'[1] Lehmann believes (without sufficient proof) that Christian ethics is somehow uprooted if it consists in reflection upon the question: what *ought* or *should* I do, or what am I *required* to do, or what is *good* for me to do, as a believer in Jesus Christ and a member of His church? Thus, he *verbally* begins with the conclusion he seeks to establish, namely, that there is no gap between ethical claim and ethical act in the Christian life.

But, of course, there is no such thing as Christian ethics if God's action in laying His gracious claim upon human life and effectuating it in and through the *koinonia* is the same as all the ethical decisions and acts that take place in the church. The Divine claim and the human ethical act cannot be telescoped; nor can: What shall or should I do? be telescoped into: What am I to do? The ways of God and the ways of man must be juxtaposed 'inconfusedly' even if 'inseparably' in the church

principles that are empty until Scripture is interpreted). My own earlier work on Christian ethics does not subordinate the systematic to the genetic approach in Christian ethical analysis or beg the basic question about ethics as a theological discipline, any more than Lehmann does when he begins to do Christian ethics by introducing the very concept of situational ethics from an interpretation of the Corinthian Letters (p. 32) and the terms *koinonia* and 'mature manhood' from an extended discussion of Ephesians 3-5 (p. 48f). By affirming that it does, Lehmann only avoids fundamental discussion of the basic theological categories in Christian ethics. Thus he avoids instructing me, and possibly receiving instruction.

[1] p. 25.

no less than in parabolic images.[1] Therefore a 'gap' which any ethics must acknowledge comes to expression, in Lehmann, in the relation between the ethical and the empirical reality of the church.[2] The actual church is only (but definitely) 'a *laboratory* of the living word', 'a *bridgehead* of maturity'.[3] The *ecclesia*, as Brunner says, is only *as real as* its faith and love and hope, and *as real as* its fellowship of concern for one another.[4] There is a tension 'between the hiddenness and the visibility of the *koinonia* in the world'.[5] The *koinonia* that is really real is 'God's fellowship-creating *mystery*'.[6] It is not there simply to be indicated by sight to sight. Lehmann rightly avoids any dualism between the hidden and the visible character of the church; but he does this by saying that these two realities of the church are 'dynamically and dialectically related in and through God's action in Christ, whose headship of the church makes the church at once the context and the custodian of the secret of the maturity of humanity'.[7]

Perhaps, the mystery of a 'dynamic', 'dialectical' relation between the hidden reality of the church and its inconfusedly but inseparably related empirical reality is sufficient for there to be Christian ethical reflection and action. Doubtless the question: What *am* I to do? contains such a dynamic, dialectical relation between the 'shall' or 'ought' aspect of its meaning and the determination of the human will in the *koinonia* by what God is doing in the world. This seems clearly to be Lehmann's meaning in what he says about the 'sign' character and the 'indicative' character of Christian moral action. In the *koinonia*, ethics is 'always fundamentally in an *indicative* rather than in an *imperative* situation'[8]; but this means '*indicative* [I take it, in the sense of pointing] rather than *verifiable*'.[9]

There is, Lehmann writes, 'also an imperative pressure exerted by an indicative situation. The "ought" factor cannot be ignored in ethical theory', only the 'ought' factor is not primary in the context of Christian ethics.[10] The hidden reality of the *koinonia* lays a claim, an imperative, upon its empirical reality; it judges the actual lives of its members. Why, then, is not precisely this relationship between the 'ought factor' and the actual life of the church better indicated by posing the

[1] p. 90.   [2] p. 68f.   [3] p. 131 (italics added).   [4] p. 50 n.
[5] p. 53 n.   [6] p. 58 (italics added).   [7] p. 72.   [8] p. 131.
[9] p. 112.   [10] p. 131.

question: What *ought* I to do as a disciple of Christ and a member of His *koinonia*? Or: What *should* I do as witness to 'the signs which point to and point up what God is doing in the world'?[1] Or: What *shall* I do to signify that what God is still doing in the world and in the churches was decisively done in Jesus Christ? Certainly there has been no Christian ethics that has used the more ordinary preceptual, normative terminology of ethics that has failed to say that the fundamental meaning of the 'right' and the 'good' comes from the participation of our moral reasoning itself in the grace and truth God has done and is doing in the world. All that Lehmann avoids is the notion that the chief cornerstone of Christian ethics is laid in the 'weak, dull and lifeless wouldings' of human beings toward the attainment of their own airy 'shouldings'.[2] The price paid for this accomplishment is, I suggest, that he greatly fore-shortens the Christian *ethical* analysis into which otherwise he would have been imperatively drawn.

Lehmann seems obsessed with removing from Christian ethics any suggestion that its proper business is 'trying to prescribe how Christians ought to behave'. He is correct, of course, in some bad senses of that expression. Still the ethicist is engaged in a 'reflective analysis' in which he endeavours 'to rethink what the Christian faith implies, as regards their [Christians'] behaviour'.[3] But the unqualified statement that in the Christian context 'ethics [can] now be a *descriptive* discipline'[4] is not only contradicted by the vast difference and dialectical relation between the hidden and the empirical reality of the *koinonia*. It is also well calculated to stifle the elaborations of those implications for behaviour.

Perhaps this is the place to indicate that there is a good deal of cheap *koinonia*-ethics abroad in the land for which Professor Lehmann, of course, is not entirely responsible, and to which his book gives little encouragement. It is too frequently said (in order to cut short the analysis of *Christian* ethical *concepts*) that Karl Barth changed the title of his *Christian Dogmatics* to *Church Dogmatics* very early in the writing of it; and some people (who have not read him enough or pondered him deeply enough) do not know that, in substance, Karl Barth could readily have changed the title back again. For Christ is the

[1] p. 112.   [2] Jonathan Edwards: *Treatise on the Religious Affections.*
[3] p. 23.   [4] p. 14.

Head of the body. As Barth says, 'The being of the community is a predicate of His being'[1]; He is not a predicate of the being of the community, of the church or the *koinonia*. 'Our fellowship is with the Father and with His Son Jesus Christ'[2]; our fellowship is not with the fellowship or with the *koinonia* or primarily with one another in it. Instead the *koinonia* is a group of joint-shareholders defined by the nature of what they share, not by their sharing, their fellowship, their 'openness', *et cetera*.[3]

In this sense, Paul Lehmann knows that Christian ethics is *Christ-ian* ethics and not *koinonia*-ethics. The church is grounded in 'the inaugural act of God'; it 'comes upon the historical scene as the answer of the disciples to that which God during the earthly life of Jesus had done in and through him'.[4] The *koinonia* is a predicate of Him; not He a predicate of the community. Because the 'new fellowship-reality' is first and basically 'between Jesus Christ and the believers', Lehmann in fact introduces the term *koinonia* for the first time in the main body of the text with the apparent tentativeness it deserves: 'We might, therefore, say that Christian ethics is *koinonia ethics*. . . .'[5] And when he sticks close to Scripture he defines the *koinonia* as '*the fellowship-creating reality* of Christ's presence in the world'.[6] He stresses that the '*head* of the body' and 'the *centre* of the fellowship' are interchangeable figures; and proves this interchangeability by reference to the 'I am' passage in the Fourth Gospel where Christ speaks of the love, than which there is none greater, by which He lays down His life.[7] Christ is the spirit whose flesh is the church. 'Where Jesus Christ is, there is the *koinonia*', Lehmann writes. One has lost his sense for the ethical reality of the *koinonia* in the world if and when he reverses this and says, 'Where the church is, there is Jesus Christ'.[8]

If it is held clearly and firmly in mind that Jesus Christ defines the Christian meaning of *koinonia*, then the proponent of *koinonia*-ethics will have to assume the burden of proving that this category is somehow different from and more fruitful of Christian ethical understanding than *agapé*. For the ethics of Christian love likewise affirms that love is a predicate of

[1] *C-D*. IV/2, p. 655.   [2] I John 1.3c.
[3] cf. C. H. Dodd: *The Johannine Epistles*, p. 7.
[4] p. 46.   [5] p. 47.   [6] p. 49.
[7] John 15.13, 14; and p. 52.   [8] p. 53.

Christ, not He a predicate of love in interpersonal relations. It is notable that Karl Barth, who yields to no one in the length and depth to which he explores the Christian life that is realised by the 'upbuilding' of the 'community', does not neglect to expound in this same context the concept and reality of *agapé* as the upbuilding in the individual of the mind of Christ[1]; and he exhaustively elucidates and articulates the meaning of the twofold love-commandment.[2] The criticism of Lehmann implied at this point is not that he seems without argument to set *koinonia*-ethics against *agapé*-ethics. The criticism is not that Lehmann refuses to enter into collaboration or dialogue with *agapé*-ethics in order that our common knowledge of the meaning of the Christian life may be advanced. It is rather that he foreshortens the elaboration of *koinonia*-ethics (and consequently of the *agapé* meaning of this) to such an extent that it may be prized for not being an ethic at all, i.e. for containing little clarification of the Christian moral requirement and only indications of the Christian context of ethics.

It seems to be one thing for Karl Barth to treat: 'Dogmatics as Ethics'[3]; another thing for Paul Lehmann to write about: Ethics as Dogmatics. In Barth there is no less ethics than dogmatics; no less elaboration of the ethical claim than there is articulation of the context. Therefore he says more about the 'actions and abstentions' that dogmatic ethics implies. Had Lehmann more fully elucidated ethics in the Christian context he would have fallen into saying more about what the Christian 'may and can and must' do. The last word in that Barthian refrain is an imperative word! It (or other words indicating the Divine claim) is just as necessary in a Christian ethics rooted in dogmatics as are words indicating that human freedom is rooted in God's permission (the basis of what the Christian 'may' do) or in the reality and power of His action (the basis of what the Christian 'can' do). But to say so much about the divine command would have seemed to Lehmann too preceptual! Instead, then, of continuing earnestly to press on in disciplined reflection upon what Christ teaches us *agapé* or *koinonia* implies, Lehmann turns rather to secular expressions to illuminate the meaning of *koinonia*. It is when the *agapé* meaning of the *koinonia* is kept clear that Lehmann is most able

[1] *C-D*, IV/2, §§67, 68.   [2] *C-D*, I/2, §18.   [3] *C-D*, I/2, §22, 3.

48

to avoid going to other sources in search of its meaning, e.g. there where the meaning of 'maturity' as *self-acceptance through self-giving* is sharply contrasted with the psychological understanding of maturity as *self-realisation through self-acceptance*.[1]

2. *What God is doing*

A second statement that can be made ostensibly about ethics in a Christian context but actually and correctly about the context of Christian ethics is to say that this means obedience to what God is doing in the world.[2] In the biblical and classical sense of the word, what God is doing in the world is 'politics'. He is governing and shaping human reality according to His will. It is appropriate to Lehmann's meaning, but not an apt denotation of the full truth, to say that God is a 'politician'[3]— for Lehmann's God is something of an opportunist, more than He is a 'statesman'. There can be no 'preceptual apprehension of the will of God', he writes, not because of the complexity of the human situations in which our apprehensions take place but because of 'the complexity of the will of God itself'. The point is made simply by iteration and reiteration: 'The will of God cannot be generalised.'[4] A being of whom such a statement can be made scarcely deserves even the name of 'politician', since a politician more often shapes human life by precepts, by having a will from which the community he governs can take normative direction.

Now, any such assertion pretends to know a lot about the will of God: Lehmann means it to be absolutely true for every situation that is God's doing and for every act of the will of God. He may be correct. If so, however, it is not because of a proper notion of the freedom of God. If God's transcendence is His freedom that cannot be prevented from making His will and acts immanent, and immanent in particular occasions, this same freedom cannot be supposed to have placed upon it the limitation that God cannot act generally or characteristically. If God can bind Himself in steadfast faithfulness to the particular, He can bind Himself in steadfast faithfulness in a general way. That would seem, indeed, to be part of the meaning of steadfastness, and of God's fidelity to His creatures through His statesmanship or His rulership. Lehmann derogates upon the freedom of God to bind the world to Himself in a general way

[1] p. 16. [2] Ch. 3. p. 83. [4] p. 77.

or in one or some ways rather than others, and thereby to claim certain and not a variety of responses from disciples of Christ and members of His *koinonia*. It is, therefore, footless theological argument (and it is one more of Lehmann's iterations) for him to dismiss all edification from the Reformer's doctrine of the 'threefold office of the law', on the ground that they were 'led by this route back to a preceptual reading of the law'. And there is a circular argument (i.e. no argument at all) disguised in the assertion that here the Reformers fell 'below the level' of their best insights.[1]

As for Lehmann's own view, he draws from Aristotle the *definition* that 'politics is activity, and reflection upon activity, which aims at and analyses what it takes to make and to keep *human* life human in the world'. He adds to this what he calls a *description*, which the Bible supplies, to the effect that 'what it takes to make and keep human life human in the world is "The unsearchable riches of Christ . . ." '.[2] But why does not Lehmann say more about the meaning of the word 'human?' Particularly if he were to derive the meaning of this word from what is entailed in the unsearchable riches of Christ in a fashion that does not just wrap an enigma in a mystery but undertakes to say fully what this means, then he would give us a *definition*, and likely a normative one implying imperatives and precepts. We would have been told something more about God's characteristic way of dealing with men than that he—habitually and generally!—plays peek-a-boo from behind the trees in the forest along the road of human history.

This, perhaps crude, metaphor is surely not greatly different from Lehmann's description of *koinonia* ethics as 'a concrete, relational ethic in which the possibilities and the actualities of the human situation are continually breaking down and continually running out into what God is doing to put them together again. . . . But if one does believe and live by the fact that God is picking up the pieces, it is incumbent upon one to be clear about where and what the pieces are.' How far is this from the second of Lehmann's 'dismal alternatives'—an 'absolutistic ethic' or a 'thoroughgoing ethical capriciousness or relativism'?[3] In this account of the ethics we know in Christian revelation, has not Christ become a predicate of the pieces? It is left for Lehmann to dare to call this *characteristic*

[1] p. 78 n.　　　[2] p. 85.　　　[3] p. 143.

of God: 'in the light of God's *characteristic* behaviour there is never any one way as against all others for dealing with any human situation'; and to glory in the fact that 'God is not really so devoid of imagination as that'.[1] Since God's 'characteristic' behaviour means that He can be, and likely is, behind two or three trees at once, there is never any one way for Christians to do what he is doing.

Barth can take ethics more seriously than Lehmann precisely because his theology is more adequate. While for Barth God is free (as Lehmann seems to say most of all and hence to be concerned with the exceptional all the time), He has also made Himself known quite historically in Jesus Christ. Jesus Christ becomes the datum for the moral life of a Christian in Barth in a way that He does not for Lehmann. In Him is all we know about the humanity of God (theology) and the humanity of man (anthropology). This is also all we are given to know about the freedom of God, i.e. His freedom to bind Himself to the world and the world to Himself. By contrast, God's freedom in Lehmann is simply an autonomous theological speculation drawn from this world of rapid change. While there remains the possibility in Barth of entirely novel, free acts of God, there is a shape to the gospel of God and a shape to His action that enables us to reflect upon it for our knowledge into God and for our knowledge into the shape of Christian moral action.

3. *Keeping Human Life Human* (*mature*)

The third statement to be made partly about ethics in a Christian context but still chiefly and correctly about the context of Christian ethics is that it is response to what God is doing in the world to keep human life *human*. 'To keep life *human*' says not much more than 'what God is doing in the world' until we are told what it means. The crucial ethical qualification of what Lehmann means by 'human' is given by the New Testament meaning of 'maturity' and of the 'new humanity'. 'The fruit of this divine activity is human maturity, the wholeness of every man and of all men in the new humanity inaugurated and being fulfilled by Jesus Christ in the world.'[2] The question to be raised later on is whether 'wholeness' controls the meaning of 'maturity' and of the human; or 'maturity'

[1] p. 141.   [2] p. 124.

51

in its New Testament sense, the meaning of 'wholeness'. The latter is the intention if not the achievement of the author.

In any case, we must keep clear that 'making human life *human*', 'maturity' and the 'new man' are Lehmann's three synonymous ethical terms. If one may say so, the 'mature manhood' or 'growing up' spoken of in Ephesians 4.13-16 is the norm; and to this, in turn, 'the measure of the stature of the fulness of Christ' gives normative definition. The Christian moral norm is in the given; the gift is the norm. The imperative and the indicative coinhere in Christ.

Yet for some strange reason Lehmann insists that 'Christian ethics is oriented towards revelation rather than toward morality. . . . [It] *aims, not at morality but at maturity*. The mature life is the fruit of Christian faith. Morality is a by-product of maturity.'[1] Either he makes here a merely *verbal* distinction between 'ethics' and 'morality'; or else he does not quite believe, with Barth, that Dogmatics is Ethics and for this reason he allows revelation and morality (or ethics) to fall apart. The first of these alternative interpretations seems to me to be closer to the author's intention, since everywhere *the ethical* or *the ethical reality* means *the mature*, the new in Christ, *the human*. The second of these interpretations, however, sums up the disaster that befalls Lehmann's ethics.

At issue here is not the ordinary and more than verbal distinction between morals or morality (social and individual behaviour) and ethics (the 'science' or knowledge of right conduct). Rather, the 'ethical' is somehow quite non-normative, non-preceptual and un-principled and it allows for no use of the value-terminology (the 'right' or the 'good') which is to be found in all ethics other than Christian ethics in Lehmann's understanding of it, and with which 'morality' abounds. 'Christian ethics is primarily concerned not with the good but with the will of God; it aims at maturity, not at morality.'[2]

Emil Brunner's definition, 'The good is what God wills' and his statement that 'the Good has its basis and its existence solely in the will of God',[3] have already started down the slippery slope toward preceptual theological ethics because of his use of the word 'good'. The same is true of Karl Barth's use of the word 'good', whom Lehmann wishes to revise in this significant respect. He begins by appealing to Barth's state-

[1] p. 54. [2] p. 121. [3] *The Divine Imperative*, p. 53.

ment that another word—the word 'ethics'—has no meaning in itself to which an author must be bound in his use of it: 'No concept possesses *as such* an absolutely general and intrinsically binding meaning, including the term, Ethics'. Lehmann then proceeds to affirm the same thing of Barth's use of value terminology in his Christian ethics, e.g. in the question Barth raises: 'What is the *Good* in and above all alleged goodness of human behaviour?'[1] Since the word 'good' has no binding meaning, no one is bound to use it in his ethics. So Barth uses it, and Lehmann does not. But then it should be noticed that Lehmann thinks *not* using this word entails something of substantive importance in Christian ethics. This turns out to be more than a verbal matter. The problem of the *Good* is 'extrinsic to the proper concern of a Christian ethic'. Moreover, Lehmann is enough of a disciple of Barth for him to want to loosen the usage of the word 'good' from Barth's own discussion of ethics. He calls this usage 'a residual influence' upon him 'of the classical and critical tradition in ethics'.[2]

One need not enter upon a merely verbal dispute—so long as it is merely verbal. If, however, anything of substantive import is entailed in Lehmann's decision not to use the word 'good' and Barth's decision to use it, then this must be called a residual influence of *the ethical problem* upon Barth's discussion—or better, it is a product of the extra-ordinary earnestness with which he pursues his reflection upon the ethical implications of Christian dogmatics. Concerning the statement in the Gospels that 'there is none good but one, that is God', Karl Barth remarks that 'to receive this truth is not to reject and abandon the question of *the goodness of human action. It is only with this truth that we take it up.*'[3] It is true that under the doctrine of God (where Lehmann says[4] Barth 'located' ethics, neglecting the rest), Karl Barth gives extended analysis simply of the proposition that 'there is no good which is not obedience to God's command'.[5] This is the source and the extent of Lehmann's ethics of 'freedom in obedience'. However, Karl Barth's undertaking for the entirety of Christian ethics requires another statement: '*there must be seen and demonstrated the fact and extent of the existence of good human action* under the lord-

---

[1] pp. 272-3. [2] p. 273 n. [3] *C-D.*, II/2, p. 574 (italics added).
[4] p. 271. [5] *C-D*, II/2, p. 541.

ship and efficacy of the divine command'.[1] Lehmann does not give or seek to fulfil such a description of the task of Christian ethics.

Instead, he separates *the ethical* from the good, revelation from morality. The reason given for this refusal to deal with morality, and for not exploring fully what this may mean even as a 'byproduct' of orientation upon *the ethical*, upon maturity' is the fact that 'the actuality of the new humanity in Christ, is the 'immediate' and 'direct' theological presupposition of what can only be called an *instant* Christian ethics. All one needs is to dwell in and say forth the context, and discern God's politics in the world, though even from this point of view it is not at all apparent why any and all statements about 'humanity in general' must be taken to mean 'humanity apart from Christ' and opposed to *particularistic* indications of 'the new humanity in Christ'.[2] Therefore, Lehmann concludes, 'Christian thinking about ethics finds it beside the point to take up the question of the nature of an act and of the relation between the nature of an act and the nature of the good'.[3] Thus, he again gives himself the conclusion that Christian ethics overcomes the fault of all other ethics, in that no gap appears between the nature of action and the nature of the good; this is one of the advantages of beginning and remaining with the given. Such a Christian ethics is, indeed, dynamically 'on the move' and 'more informal' according to the root meaning of that last word: unconstructed,[4] that is, more unstructured, and reflection about the moral life more undisciplined, than any analysis of the moral claims upon human behaviour 'in terms of a progressive movement from the partial to the perfect'.[5] That last word opens up gaps and is incipiently preceptual.

It is true, of course, that 'Be ye therefore mature' may be a better translation of Matt. 5.48 than 'Be ye therefore perfect'. But the term 'maturity' in its New Testament meaning also opens up a gap between the nature of human acts and the nature of mature human conduct, unless a way can be found to avoid going into that subject. I suggest that Paul Lehmann succeeds in leaving his Christian ethics 'unconstructed' by shifting contexts. This is accomplished by yet another translation of Matt. 5.48, with but one word inserted in a parenthesis:

[1] *C-D*, III/4, p. 6 (italics added).
[2] p. 121.   [3] pp. 121-2.   [4] p. 122 and n.   [5] p. 122.

54

'men will be mature (whole) as their Father in heaven is'.[1]

Instead of articulating more fully the meaning of maturity for the actions and abstensions implied in and for Christian discipleship, Professor Lehmann turns from the Christian to a secular context for the illumination of the meaning of this category and for a demonstration of the way it comprehends the very texture of human existence. That texture tends to become the substantive of which Christ is predicate. His *language* indicates the emergence of other controlling thought-forms than are quite warranted by the 'temple', 'body' and 'vine' imagery or metaphors in the New Testament, which ought always to be understood in terms of *agapé* covenant-relationships (and not *vice versa*): 'A pattern of integrity in and through interrelatedness.'[2] 'For maturity *is* integrity in and through interrelatedness which makes it possible for each individual member of an organic whole to be himself in to-getherness, and in togetherness each to be himself. This is maturity.'[3] 'The thrust of the *koinonia* into the world means that all ordinary conduct is *socialised* rather than *universalised*.'[4] 'The societal character of Christian faith and life.'[5]

After saying that the *koinonia* is 'a fellowship of maturity in love',[6] Lehmann readily puts 'whole' for 'Head' or 'Lord' in the explanation of the meaning of this: 'a fellowship in which each individual functions properly himself in relation to the whole, and the whole functions properly in so far as each individual is related to it'.[7] He explains Luther's 'through love being changed into each other' and Calvin's 'let us be whatever we are for each other' by 'organic inter-relational differentiation'.[8]

Of course, in the midst of 'part-whole', 'part-part' and ' "one" confronts the "other" ' language, a more adequate Christian contextual language often succeeds in re-emerging: a 'society in which all the parts properly function insofar as all the parts, one way or another, minister Christ to all the other parts'.[9] But why be so hesitant in saying what 'ministering Christ' may mean in ethical theory and moral actions or abstensions? Until an ethics in a Christian context is articulated more reflectively, the language of secular contextualism will

[1] p. 123.   [2] p. 54.   [3] p. 55.
[4] p. 56.   [5] p. 61.   [6] p. 61.
[7] p. 62.   [8] p. 66.   [9] p. 68.

tend to fill the vacuum left by—indeed exhibited by—repeated inarticulate reference to what God is doing in the world to keep human life human. Doubtless, the church is 'the *context* and the *custodian* of the secret of the maturity of humanity' and 'the *starting point* for the Christian life and for our thinking about Christian ethics'.[1] But spinning on the spot is not the only alternative to imagining vainly that the Christian can make another beginning or that Christian ethics could ever reflect itself away from this ground in which it is nourished.

One need not, and I am not competent to, quarrel with Lehmann's translation of 1 Cor. 10.16-17 in which he finds the phrases 'fellowship of belonging' and 'we are what we are in belonging'.[2] Nor need we forget all his passages in which the biblical meaning of human maturity is expounded. Still, one can wish that Lehmann had continued along the line of his own requirement for an 'ethics of depth', i.e. 'an *ethical analysis which tries to spell out what is involved in* human maturity as the final fruit of being "firmly fixed in love . . . able to grasp . . . how wide and deep and long and high is the love of Christ" '.[3] Then would there have been more contact with the entire tradition of Christian ethical reflection. Then, I suspect, we might have heard something about *the law of Christ*, or some reasonable facsimile thereof; more about what a Christian can and may and must do; and more about the actions and abstentions implied for Christian discipleship. Instead we are told—and I venture to believe that such passages will prove especially meaningful to contemporary readers in and out of the churches—that 'maturity is the full development in a human being of the power to be truly and fully himself in being fully related to others who also have the power to be truly and fully themselves'.[4] In what direction would *you* look for an explication of ethics in *that* context? Moreover, it is ethics developed within this context that is apt to be productive of an indefinitely variable, dynamic, *instant* ethics so long as there are no imperative formulations brought against the concrete context and no preceptual claims made upon the texture of relationships. Ethics in a Christian context (or, for that matter, any ethics) is required and able to be far richer in ethical implications. It will be productive of knowledge *into God*, knowledge

---

[1] p. 72 (italics added).   [2] p. 100 n.
[3] Eph. 3.18-21 and p. 101 (italics added).   [4] p. 101.

into human existence and knowledge *into ethics*—if these are not too authentically Barthian statements for Lehmann to accept. Even 'wholeness' and 'inter-relatedness', when taken with utmost philosophical seriousness as the standard and definition of goodness, have produced a great tradition in the rational analysis of moral action and many great systems of ethics; but then no one pretends to have abolished the tension between the ethical claim and the ethical act, or that ethics, as such, has any business other than articulating exactly that.

The truth is that in Lehmann's ethics the development of a normative ethics of wholeness is inhibited by the degree to which Christian categories prevail, and the development of a Christian ethics is frustrated by his readiness to turn elsewhere for the meaning of maturity. In order to see quite clearly, however, that Lehmann's minimum notion of wholeness is drawn from the philosophy of self-realisation developed in the modern era, with a liberal dosage of Freudianism, one need only ask: why is it more 'mature' for a person to develop organically in interpersonal relationships than for his maturity to be determined by wholly other claims, commands, obligations imperatives, and by what's right? This is not a question to be begged, or one to be answered in Christian ethics by imparting the assumptions of the present age.

The business of Christian ethics is to exhibit and formulate the implications of 'mature manhood' in the New Testament understanding of it as these may bear on all the concrete 'wholes' in the world in which men are called to discipleship. Lehmann definitely tends to interpret 'mature manhood' in the light of secular 'wholeness' rather than interpreting the wholeness into which we must grow up as maturity measured by the stature of the fullness of Christ. The evidence for this is sufficient to call gravely into question his claim that 'the contextual character of Christian ethics is not derived from an application to the Christian *koinonia* of a general theory of contextualism'.[1]

To see this one has only to place what Lehmann means by 'human' alongside of what Karl Barth means by the Word. When Barth takes up specific ethical questions, such as 'the humanity of human work', the question he asks is whether and to what extent it is human in the special sense of 'fellow human',[2] and this term in turn takes its entire meaning from a

[1] p. 15. [2] *C-D*, III/4, p. 535.

57

doctrine of creation and of the nature of man as a being created by Jesus Christ and toward Jesus Christ. An image of this is to be found in the creation of man and woman toward one another; and this has to be spelled out in Christian ethics. For Barth Christology is not the same as anthropology; and even Christocentric anthropology is not the same as Christology. For Lehmann, 'dogmatics as ethics' is largely restricted to Christology or Theology; and this gives him no protection against unacknowledged anthropological insights drawn from non-Christian sources, to wit, secular contextualism. Thus, for example, trust, belonging, openness and wholeness provide in large measure the meaning of humanity in the relations between the sexes in Lehmann's views, while Barth elaborates the Christocentric meaning of man-womanhood as our creation in and for 'fellow humanity', which gives meaning to the belonging and the fidelity required by our creator.

The primacy of a general theory of contextualism begins to assert itself even in Lehmann's discussion of the theological and ecclesiological context of Christian ethics, and of the methodology for developing the ethics required or made possible by this context. It becomes even more plainly evident when we come to questions of application and to what is said in this volume concerning 'the contextual character of Christian ethics'. We shall have to take the author at his word in reporting a recent 'discovery' of 'the extent to which my own approach to ethics has been affected by the intellectual climate so formatively shaped, if not inaugurated by, [William] James'[1]; and this raises the crucial question about just how formative the Christian biblical context or the faith and ethics of the Reformation have been for Lehmann's ethical theory.

4. *Christocentric ethics*

Christian ethics is *ex animo* an ethics of messianism.[2] This means it is Christological. Granting that the Messiah 'is unintelligible apart from the covenant community, the corporate structure of God's activity in the world',[3] Lehmann devotes an entire chapter to the proposition that the *koinonia* is unintelligible apart from the Messiah, and He no predicate of it.

This leads to a final cluster of three statements to be made chiefly and correctly about the Christological context of

[1] p. 192 n. Cf. p. 195 n.   [2] p. 104.   [3] p. 58.

Christian ethics, but whose implications for ethics in that context are as yet uncertain. These are statements about 'the divine behaviour', Lehmann writes; and he adds immediately, 'and thus also of human behaviour'[1]: (1) Christian ethics has a Trinitarian basis, it is rooted in the triune *economy* of God's action; (2) its context is redemption as this is understood under the Threefold Office of Christ, His prophetic, regal and priestly functions; and (3) the nature and direction of the human fulfilment of which Christians speak is oriented upon the Second Adam, the Second Advent. Together, these Christological affirmations indicate the environment and the prospect of Christian behaviour.

Lehmann several times points out an advantage for the enterprise of Christian ethics in keeping these doctrines—or the reality to which they point—steadily in mind. The trinitarian formulation is 'an important traditional safeguard against basing ethics upon *theological anthropology*'.[2] The significance of a theology and ethics of messianism is exactly that it protects against a 'metaphysical surrender',[3] against a natural, ontological or anthropological environment for ethics. The doctrine of the Second Adam, in particular, 'fortifies the Christological focus' by removing 'the last possibility of a surreptitious resort to *anthropology* in Christian ethical reflection'.[4] And later Lehmann writes, he thinks tellingly against John Bennett, that 'a *theological anthropology* is simply insufficient to support the method and substance of Christian ethical reflection'.[5]

He who would pick any bones with this must first understand it. Does Lehmann reject anthropology in general from among the bases of Christian ethical reflection, or only general anthropology? Does he only oppose surreptitious resort to

---

[1] p. 105.   [2] p. 109 n. (italics added).
[3] p. 112 n.   [4] p. 120 (italics added).
[5] p. 154 (italics added). Lehmann's discussion at this point (pp. 148-59) 'of the concept of middle axioms' developed by Dr J. H. Oldham and Professor John Bennett (and his discussion of Bennett's unpublished paper 'Principles and the Situation') is vitiated by his supposition that the *chief* point about the theory of natural law or the concept of middle axioms was to establish 'a common link between the believer and the non-believer' (p. 148). I should have said that the chief point was how the believer himself and the community of believers are to arrive at any guidance for Christian moral and social action, whether or not this links them with non-believers in a common enterprise. The question, therefore, of Christian anthropology or of a Christian doctrine of creation or of the Christian natural law, or of the 'orders' or of rule-agapism, etc., are questions *within* Christian theological ethics, not apologetic ethics.

anthropology, or as well any elaboration of *theological* anthropology? Among the options in theological anthropology is an elaboration of a Christocentric understanding of the nature of man; and Lehmann himself makes reference to Barth's '*special* anthropology of Jesus Christ . . . the *norm* of *all anthropology*'.[1]

One can fruitfully inquire into the dependent or independent relationship, surreptitious or otherwise, between general anthropology and Barth's Christocentric theological anthropology as a basis for ethics. But since Lehmann develops no Christian doctrine of man as one ingredient in the environment of Christian ethics, this question cannot fruitfully be raised with him. He does refer to a 'dialectical relation between the "second Adam" and the "first Adam" in the shaping of the new humanity'[2]; but he nowhere tells us anything about the nature of one pole of that dialectic, namely, the 'first Adam'. This would require a statement concerning the nature of *the man* ('Adam') as this may be understood of the 'first' from the point of view of the 'second Adam'.

Here again, however, it may be observed that the fact that Lehmann elaborates no Christocentric theological anthropology does not mean that he is innocent of anthropological insights, or that these are without significant weight in his ethics. It only means that the anthropological underpinning of a secular theory of contextualism comes to fill the vacuum. Indeed, in his resolve to stick with the ultimates of a theology of messianism, Lehmann is without the protection against independent anthropological insights (which for him are the structures of a structureless understanding of the human situation) which Barth secures by unhesitatingly basing a large part of his ethics on a carefully worked-out theological anthropology. The wording 'mature (whole)' was one indication of where Lehmann's meaning comes from. Another mis[?]translation of a New Testament verse will indicate that, taken so alone, the Second Adam as the aim and prospect of 'maturity' in its Christian ethical meaning fails quite definitely to remove the last possibility of a surreptitious resort to anthropology in Christian ethical reflection. 'When God is everything to everyone (I Cor. 15.29) then men will be "like God", that is, everything to everyone.'[3] Being like God means being everything to everyone; the advantage of saying it this way is that no one

[1] p. 119.   [2] p. 154.   [3] p. 106 n.

could possibly give you a prescription for that! Being like God in any Christian qualitative sense would, of course, immediately admit of preceptual understanding of God's claim, of the prospect or *telos* of human maturity, of what God is doing in the world to make human life human.

In this connexion, it may be noted that Lehmann makes the astonishing and quite incorrect statement that 'Barth includes ethics under the doctrine of God, not the doctrine of man'.[1] He knows better, assiduous student of Barth that he is; and anyone who knows of the existence of *C-D*, III/4 knows better. The fact is that there is an ethical articulation of *every* doctrine in Barth's *Dogmatics*; and that our knowledge *into God, into man.* and *into ethics* are all fully explored and fully Christocentric. Anthropology is no further removed from Christology than Theology is, or for that matter Ethics with its statements about actions and abstensions that Christians may and can and must perform insofar as they are disciples of Christ and members of his *koinonia*.

Here a final comment is in order. It is that Lehmann has particular need for that part of Barth's dogmatic ethics where he seems only to locate ethics within the doctrine of God. For here the freedom and uniqueness of the Divine command and claim are emphasised.[2] (Even here, the words 'command' and 'claim' are used, and not is-language alone.) In his *Dogmatics* taken as a whole, however, Barth stresses as well what is entailed for man in God's binding Himself to the world and the world to Himself; he does not hesitate to discourse upon the doctrines of creation and the nature of man, and in this connexion to elaborate a 'special ethics' entailed in all this.[3] This 'special ethics' gets quite specific, before ever Barth surrounds and locates an 'exception' which is steadfastly preserved in its nature as an exception by its environment in Christian ethical analysis.

In a section entitled 'The Protection of Life', Barth writes that 'The command of respect for human life . . . is not a law but a direction for service.'[4] It is, however, a *definite* directive, under which Barth analyses such problems as suicide, killing another person, abortion, euthanasia, self-defence, capital punishment, and killing in war. 'Thou shalt not kill', writes Barth, 'reaches us in such a way that in all the detailed prob-

[1] p. 271. [2] *C-D*, II/2. [3] *C-D*, III/4. [4] *C-D*, III/4, p. 433.

61

lems which may arise we cannot exclude the exceptional case and yet we cannot assert too sharply that it is genuinely exceptional. In other words, we cannot overemphasise the arguments against it . . .'[1] even when we judge that in an exception to the rule that life should always be sustained there may be a call of God. Moreover, even *in* the exception the rule is applied: 'God as the Lord of life may further its protection even in the *strange form* of its conclusion and termination rather than in its [immediate?] preservation and advancement.'[2] Even so, this exceptional service, 'this exceptional case can and should be envisaged and accepted only as such, only as *ultima ratio*, only as highly exceptional, and only with the greatest reserve on the exhaustion of all other possibilities'.[3] In other words, Barth asks and attempts to answer the question: What is the meaning of the forbidden self-destruction, or the prohibited killing? His answer to this question surrounds and locates the exception and sustains it as a genuine exception (so much so that the more one reads Barth and ponders his writings on special ethics, the more 'the exception' itself will be discovered to be a case of specific application).

By contrast, Lehmann can write, and does write, 'Christianity *specialises* in the exception'. He says that an exception which 'suspends the rule' and does not 'fall securely under normative generalisation' is the truly significant case because it breaks challengingly with the surrounding normative context and 'breaks fresh ethical ground'.[4] In contrast, Barth's 'exception' continues to bear the burden placed upon it by the acknowledged general validity of right conduct in the matter to which exception is allowed. Indeed, an ethical exception cannot, by definition, exist unless this is the case. No ethics can specialise in it. Lehmann, however, can write of 'the "rule" of forgiveness' that: 'Here was a "rule" which was not a rule', it 'could only be applied as a suspension of itself'[5]—thus building his ethics upon a plainly self-contradictory notion of an exception, and withdrawing everything he seemed to say when earlier he wrote: 'The statement "God forgives" is a theological statement that does imply necessarily an ethical statement, i.e. that "Men should deal with one another as God deals with

[1] p. 400.
[2] p. 398 (italics added). What is this if it is not rule-agapism and 'love's casuistry' that does not seek to overleap principles?
[3] p. 398.   [4] pp. 243-4.   [5] p. 245.

them", viz. forgive one another.'[1] That would seem not ever to be suspended in application, whether or not it is called a 'rule' or a 'rule which was not a rule' (whatever that may mean).

Here, however, the point is not the ethics that may be located under the doctrine of God, or such ultimates as justification. It is rather the question whether Christian ethics does not require also an ethics located under the doctrines of creation and man. It is the question whether there is a Christian ethic if about all that can be said by or to husband and wife who are in the depths of moral predicament is: 'If what God is doing in the world has anything to do with what man is doing in the world, it is His next move!'[2]

Professor James M. Gustafson has written that Lehmann's book 'could be reviewed instructively as an emendation of Barth's theology and ethics'.[3] If it is an emendation, Barth's ethics is here considerably reduced—and not in length only but in indispensable moments for Christian ethical reflection. After the statement, near the end of the book, that 'A context for conscience concludes with a conscience for that context', the author was troubled for the second time by the apparent emptiness and circularity of his 'conclusion' (which is surely ethically impoverished whether this be conscience in a Christian or a secular context). He asked whimsically: 'Has the mountain merely laboured to bring forth a mouse? Or is this the mouse which gnaws the lion free?'[4] He leans good-humouredly to the latter opinion. Leaning as I do toward the former one, I may say that the mouse has gnawed Christian conscience free from a good deal that is necessary if there is to be any such thing as Christian ethics.

Lehmann's understanding of Christian ethics, however, may be said to be a characteristically American statement of the subject. This is truly 'A theology for . . .' the Committees on Christian Social Concerns. For in American Protestant theology we do not so much resist 'natural' justice as opposed to 'revealed' ethics or revealed ethics as opposed to the ethics of natural law. Behind this antinomy there is even greater resistance to any full-scaled articulation of ethics whether on the basis of nature or revelation or both. Barth's specific

[1] p. 239.
[2] p. 321.
[3] *Union Seminary Quarterly Review*, XIX, 3 (March 1964), p. 262.
[4] pp. 351, and 284 n. 1.

ethics and its theological ground-work are not apt to prove any more acceptable than moral theology with *its* 'casuistry'.

B

THE CONTEXTUAL CHARACTER OF CHRISTIAN ETHICS

This, then, is a book about the context. It is a book on the doctrine of the church, on the methodology of Christian ethics, on messianism or christology, on justification, on divine and human freedom, on what God is doing in the world making for maturity and the new humanity. The volume has to be assessed in terms of the adequacy with which these theological doctrines and methods are set forth. It is only quite subordinately a book about the nature and meaning of ethics in this context.

The present writer is quite conscious of the fact that in the foregoing he may have already reflected beyond warrant upon the ethical implications that follow or do not follow from taking Lehmann's approach to Christian ethics and from this understanding of its context. The author himself makes quite clear that:

> The elaboration of what is involved in the constructive substance of a *koinonia* ethic lies beyond the scope of the present inquiry and must presuppose the methodological analysis with which these pages are concerned. Only then can a systematic exposition of the content of a Christian ethic exhibit the distinctive orientation with which the gospel provides behaviour. And only in the light of such an orientation can the meaning of forgiveness and love, of love and righteousness, of the role of law in Christian life, and of the difference which being a Christian makes in personal conduct and in social patterns and structures be intrinsically explained.[1]

If this is forthcoming in the next volume, the present reviewer will be the first to be glad he was proved wrong. From a huge furnace of doubt my hosanna will break forth! For then Christian ethic will have made great advances both in theoretical formulation and in possible application.

Nevertheless, Lehmann serves up more than a morsel of what may be expected from an ethics within his understanding of its context and method. This he does in a chapter entitled, 'The Contextual Character of Christian Ethics'. We must now turn to this chapter and to a few other places in the present

[1] p. 224.

volume where Lehmann begins to do Christian ethics. I propose first to raise one general question about the contextual character of Christian ethics. Then we will examine what Lehmann has to say about (1) the problem of truth-telling, (2) sex ethics, and (3) a Christian's participation in war, which are the three substantive moral problems discussed in this chapter.

The first question to be asked is how, by what logic, and with what justification Lehmann moves from the title of this book, 'Ethics in a Christian Context' to the title of this chapter, 'The Contextual Character of Christian Ethics'. This, of course, requires no demonstration if the transition from 'context' to 'contextual' is only grammatical. One can always turn a noun into an adjective, a substantive into a predicate, provided he means no more than and nothing different from the noun when he uses the adjectival form. In this sense, ethics in a Christian context is obviously contextual. One has said no more by using the word 'contextual' than was contained in the statement, to which I suppose no one objects, that Christian ethics is ethics in a Christian theological context. In this sense, and this sense alone, there can be no objection to the assumption that Christian ethics has contextual character. Just so, a Tillich might affirm that ethics is rooted in ontology; and, after proving that, he could speak about the ontological character of ethics provided the predicate 'ontological' contained no assumption about the content of that ethic beyond establishing the fact that 'ontology' must be its basis. There may be a wide variety of possible ethical systems, and ways of dealing with specific moral problems, that can all be called ontological; and there may be a wide variety of Christian ethical systems that are possible, and ways of dealing with specific moral problems, that could be called 'contextual' because they all agree that Christian ethics must be ethics in a Christian theological 'context'.

I am afraid, however, that Lehmann thinks he has said more than that about the nature of Christian ethics when he passes from using the noun 'context' to using the adjective 'contextual'. He seems to assume that he has said something by the word 'contextual' and yet that there is no more to prove in order to establish his notion of the contextual character of Christian ethics than has already been shown in establishing the fact that it is always ethics in a Christian context. In one sense—the grammatical sense—Christian ethics is obviously contextual; in any more significant sense, he begs the question who does not undertake to demonstrate. Is there not a simple logical and grammatical illation involved when Lehmann writes that 'when the church is the context of ethical reflection, Christian ethics becomes contextual'?[1] This is evident in only the most inconsequential, grammatical sense. But Lehmann assumes that the word 'contextual' as an attribute of Christian ethics says a good deal more than the nominative 'context' requires, and more than has been shown to be required by the primacy of Christian theology to Christian ethics.

Great minds before Lehmann have made so simple yet crucial a mistake. John Stuart Mill, for example, reasoned that since we call something 'visible' because it can be seen or 'edible' because it is eaten, so the only reason for believing a thing is 'desirable' is the fact that it is desired. If 'desirable' means no more than 'able to be desired', that is evidently established by the fact that someone desires it; but Mill clearly meant more than this by his use of the word. He meant 'worth being desired'. Just so, if 'contextual' means no more than that the ethics we are talking about is in a Christian context, that is evidently established by the fact that we are speaking of Christian ethics. But Lehmann clearly means more than this by his use of the expression 'the contextual character of Christian ethics'. No one denies that something that is desired is, in that sense, 'desirable'; or that ethics in a Christian context is, in that sense, 'contextual' ethics. No more meaning can be obtained from the adjective than there is, in the first case, in the verb or, in the second case, in the noun. Such is the simple but glaring logical mis-step that has already been made when Lehmann begins his discussion of particular problems with the aim of illustrating the contextual character of Christian ethics.

1. *The bearing of Truth-telling upon truth-telling*

Lehmann opens his discussion of the question of truth-telling by reasserting that 'a koinonia *ethic is concerned with relations and functions, not with principles and precepts*'. He reveals his unexamined assumption about 'principles', in that this contrast promptly becomes a contrast between *contextual ethics* and

[1] p. 73.

absolutist ethics.[1] He then further reveals his understanding of 'absolutist ethics' by defining an 'absolute' as *'a standard of conduct which can be and must be applied to all people in all situations in exactly the same way'*.[2] If that is the meaning of absolutes in ethics, and still further if that is the meaning of principles and precepts, then very few absolutists in ethical theory have measured up to it, and almost no defenders of moral principles have done so. Because of these faulty assumptions, we are forewarned that Lehmann may be quite mistaken when he asserts that an affirmative answer to the question, Is the Christian required to tell the truth? can only be 'based upon a conception or standard of truth which is foreign to the focus and foundations of a Christian ethic'.[3] That will have to be proved—negatively by showing that truth-telling as a principle is foreign and positively by a full exploration of the bearing, if any, of a Christian's Truth-telling upon his truth-telling.

Lehmann, of course, has no difficulty in disposing of the farcical situations in the stage-play *Nothing But the Truth* and in rejecting the pure formalism of Kant's essay *On the Supposed Right to Tell a Lie from Altruistic Motives*. He might have been led toward a sounder ethical analysis if he had taken up more seriously the position of the man Kant was trying to refute. That author believed that while it is generally a duty to tell the truth, this only applies to someone who has a right to it. Thus, he placed an *extrinsic* limitation upon the duty of truth-telling; he allowed that there were exceptions to this rule. A consideration of this viewpoint might have opened up an entire body of traditional teachings upon this subject which goes further than Kant's opponent and defines the *intrinsic* meaning of the truth in question by reference to those to whom it is due, and defines the forbidden lie as any denial of the truth (in the sense of verbal accuracy) to someone to whom the truth is due. This would have disclosed that there are very many great moral thinkers who affirm a principle of truth-telling but who are not 'absolutist' in Lehmann's restricted—I might even say, abstract, absolutist and non-contextual—meaning of that word.

Instead of asking after the meaning of truth-telling in the light of Truth-telling, or in the light of some other ethical reality, Lehmann tries 'to get at it this way: Suppose a man

[1] p. 124.   [2] p. 125.   [3] p. 125.

has a car which he wants to sell.' *Then* and only then does he ask 'situationally', 'What does it mean to tell the truth?'[1] From no number of suppositions about men who have cars to sell, or from other supposed situations of the same order, will an answer to the question of the meaning of telling the truth *arise*. Such 'cases' help to clarify the meaning in application of telling the truth to someone to whom the truth is due. They may even make it plain that there are exceptions and that there is a problem of compromise, when, for example, one must withhold or deny the truth to someone to whom it is rightfully due under ordinary circumstances, for the sake of an unusual and overriding obligation (in the case of a man who has only one car to sell, no other way of securing funds and who must pay at once for his wife's emergency operation—her *burial*, Lehmann says!). So has Christian ethics in almost all ages 'justified' theft under certain circumstances (since the right of property is not the absolute, but only charity), or assassination or war (since life is not the absolute).

Lehmann, however, begins and stays with 'the exception' which then is, of course, no exception in any reasonable meaning of the term. Specialising in the exceptional (which is, when you think about it, a quite self-contradictory vocation), he has only rules which were never rules, principles which were never principles, and a meaning for truth-telling which was never the meaning of the truth to be told in ordinary transactions. This lands him in some extraordinarily naïve arguments. For example, who (since it was not Kant or Fichte or even that playful farce) ever defined truth-telling as '*optimum verbal veracity*' in such a fashion that it is pertinent even to mention the fact that 'he might have forgotten something' about the car he is trying to sell?[2] This is not a trivial point to bring up,

---

[1] p. 128.

[2] p. 129. Note that my question is: Who ever defined truth-telling as 'optimum verbal veracity' *in such a fashion that it is pertinent even to mention the fact*, etc.? The italicised words are crucial; and Mr Lehmann omitted and took no account of these words, which are crucial, in his reply ('Critic's Corner', *Theology Today*, April 1965) to this portion of the present essay (*Theology Today*, January 1965, pp. 466-75). The whole of ethics prior to Lehmann—so far as this literature has come to my attention—establishes a significant *relation* between personal integrity and verbal integrity, and from the former it articulates the latter requirement. *This* is the issue, if Lehmann will let it be joined. The issue is whether Truth-telling has any bearing on truth-telling; and, if so, what is entailed in Christ for our knowledge *into ethics* and for truth-telling in ordinary transactions. The issue is whether Lehmann did not first *attribute* to normative ethics the absurdity of defining truth-telling as verbal veracity *alone;* and then was himself propelled to

because Lehmann places right after this supposed refutation of truth-telling as optimum verbal veracity a supposed refutation of one of 'the most ingenious and tested and tried attempts to bring an absolutist ethic into line with the actual diversity and complexity of the ethical situation', namely the distinction between the *intention* and the *action* done, with greater importance assigned to the *intention* to do or say the right thing.[1] But truth-telling is neither verbal veracity alone nor the intention alone, if it means actually communicating the truth (and, of course, intending to do so) to someone to whom the truth in question belongs.

This does mean, of course, that, in the words of Bonhoeffer, 'telling the truth must be learned' and an 'increasingly accurate knowledge of the situation is a necessary element of ethical action'.[2] Knowledge of the situation may be a necessary element, even an indispensable one, if one is to learn to tell the truth. A knowledge of the truth to be told may, indeed, only 'arise with' increased knowledge of the situation. From the situation I may also learn more about the range and depth of the truth-claims upon me. But truth-telling as a claim upon me does not 'arise from' the situation; and *a fortiori* it does not arise from the variables in situations.

To tell the truth means, Lehmann says in Bonhoeffer's phrase, to speak 'the right word' or better 'the living word'.[3] But what first and fundamentally gives meaning to the 'right' and 'living' word to be spoken is Lehmann's secular theory of contextualism. (Such it must be called, despite the author's disavowal.) In place of optimum verbal veracity or a correspondence between thought and word, he puts situational coherence as the meaning of truth-telling. 'What is *ethical* about the existing, concrete situation is that which holds it together'; and what holds the situation together, in turn, are words that make it 'possible for human beings to be open *for*

---

a like absurdity, namely, defining truth-telling as personal integrity and openness *alone*. Heretofore it has been understood that there is an important connexion between the integrities, i.e. between authentic interpersonal response and the correspondence of human speech with the mind's apprehension of (small letter) truths. It is not possible to avoid the normative requirement of (little letter) truth-telling without soaring with some assertedly 'ethical' reality above life's situations.

[1] pp. 128-9.
[2] q. p. 129.
[3] p. 129.

69

one another and *to* one another'.[1] This is the meaning of the right and living word.

Of course, it is important to stress that 'to communicate' does not mean idle talk, nor does the integrity of human communication consist solely in a correspondence between one's thought and one's words. Moreover, an aspect of integrity in communication, and perhaps the controlling dimension of it, is being 'in an actual relationship with somebody in which you give yourself to him and he gives himself to you'.[2] To tell the truth requires, it would seem, both a certain correspondence and integrity between thought and speech and a co-respondence and integrity between the speaker and other persons. Having defined an ethic of principle in this matter to mean verbal veracity alone, Lehmann proceeds to make the opposite mistake of defining truth-telling as personal co-respondence and openness alone.

This only states the problem of truth-telling, not an answer to it. The problem is whether to communicate with my neighbour, and in this sense to be true to him, I must tell him the truth in the sense that my words will need to match my thoughts and the facts. Lehmann is simply too obsessed with the exceptional case, in which in order to be true to my neighbour it may be that my words should not correspond exactly with my thoughts. There remains for him not even a derivative connexion between co-respondence with or openness to the other person and correspondence between thought and speech, which surrounds and even makes logically and actually possible the exceptional case. In contrast, the well-established analysis of the problem of truth-telling in terms of telling the truth (verbal veracity) to persons to whom the truth is due has at least this to commend it: that the *ethical* problem or the problem of veracity in both senses and the bearing of the one upon the other has been directly addressed. It is simply too easy to dismiss 'absolutism' and establish contextualism by ignoring this analysis of the meaning of telling the truth.

In passing, it may also be asked whence Lehmann gets the idea that whatever 'holds the situation together' and makes it possible for persons to be open for one another and to one another is *right* or *living* in word or in fact. Suppose I don't want to hold things together, or don't want to be open and

[1] p. 130.   [2] p. 64.

rather live otherwise. It is not obvious that I should do so. There can be no answer to this question that is not *normative* (theological or otherwise); nor can there be an answer to this question that does not open a gap between the actual concrete context and what the context *should* be. Ethics cannot be born out of any concrete 'whole' without the moral requirement or claim of 'wholeness'. Nor, for that matter, does the *indicative* theological statement, 'God forgives', imply the injunction, 'Forgive one another' without the intervention of a *normative* statement in theological ethics, 'Men *should* deal with one another as God deals with them'.[1] Neither in a secular context nor in a Christian context is it possible to formulate the ethical question as 'What *am* I to do?' Any ethics, in any context, must ask, 'What *ought* I to do?'

Lehmann fails to explore the ultimate requirement of openness of human beings for one another and to one another in its implications for truth-telling with a small 't'. If buyer and seller discover each other as human beings, 'whether much or little is told about the car, *whatever is told is the truth*'.[2] They 'do not merely transact business'. In fact it is difficult to see that they are transacting *business* at all. The transaction in which they are engaged is an ultimate one; it is interhuman communication, and in this they are true to one another.

The first thing to be said about this is that if the seller succeeds in withholding some 'truth' about the car he must also try to hide the truth about his own human 'predicament' which drove him to it; and it is hard to see how he is going to disclose or communicate himself to the other, or be open to the other, if he really succeeds in his dissimulation (which is the meaning of an effective withholding of the truth). Thus, integrity of speech and correspondence between word and thought would seem to be entailed in integrity of co-respondence between man and man, no matter how much more important the latter is than the former.

The second thing to be said is that such a radical shifting of the problem from truth-telling in 'mere business' transactions to telling forth the truth in interpersonal openness comes as close to Lehmann's definition of an 'absolute' as any principle that has ever been formulated preceptually. His language, of course, sounds thoroughly relevant, contextual, nay, even

[1] cf. p. 239.   [2] p. 130 (italics added).

71

relativistic: 'in all these relationships the truth in the words varies.'[1] But what is the 'truth' which is being communicated, what is this openness *for* and *to* one another, if it is not a standard for conduct which invariably can be and must be applied to all people and to every situation? This is the Truth that can and may and must be told unconditionally. No matter what is said in ordinary transactions, whether much or little is told about the car, whether speech is or is not an accurate reflection of the mind's apprehension of the facts about the little transactions of daily life, the fundamental thing can still be exhibited and 'whatever is told is the truth'. That last word should have been capitalised or the article italicised, to indicate the contextualist's absolute. This is abstracted from any *important* relevance to authenticity in spoken words or degrees of verbal integrity. Because Truth-telling is relevant to all it may find embodiment in many or in any ways. This is a statement of the problem of (small letter) truth-telling in human communication, no answer to it. If this is the meaning of the *koinonia* as a 'laboratory of the living word',[2] there may be in it some or even rich *nourishment* for the seeds of truth, but little ethical clarification of its meaning.

Lehmann gives one instance of contextualism *in a Christian context* to illustrate a Christian's truth-telling. This was the case of the devout woman 'who had come to be virtually a second mother' to the author, and who asked him in her extreme pain and terminal illness, 'What do the doctors say? Is there anything to be done?'[3]

Now, there's a question to deal with, and with which to test the adequacy of one's theory! In dealing with the poignant problem posed for him by his friend, Lehmann comes closest to dealing with the real moral issue and yet his analysis drives him to a place most removed from it. He says rightly that 'the point at issue here is not the celebrated ethical problem of the right of the patient to the truth'.[4] That was a reference to Joseph Fletcher's inter-personalistic—one might even say contextual—treatment of the problem of (small letter) truth-telling in his *Morals and Medicine*.[5] This would have been a far, far better position than Kant's for Lehmann to break his lances against, if he wanted to demonstrate that all the Christian

---

[1] p. 130.   [2] p. 131.   [3] p. 132.   [4] p. 132.
[5] Princeton University Press, 1954.

72

knows to do is to 'wade in and wade through' since that is what the God of the Bible who 'places little importance upon human consistency' (or, it would seem, upon His own as well) is doing 'to get His purposes accomplished'.[1]

But Lehmann is quite correct when he says that the problem of (small letter) truth-telling is *not* (only) the patient's right to the truth. It is *not* interpersonal co-respondence. It is *not* one's openness to and for others and of others to and for him. The point at issue is rather '*what*', because of all this, '*is the truth* to which the patient has a right'.[2]

Thus the decisive question was raised of the bearing of personal co-respondence upon correspondence between speech and thought about the final finite transaction of a person's dying. Now, there are far profounder sorts of veracity than verbal ones. It may be that Lehmann answered his friend's actual question but did not do so verbally. It may be that by tone or gesture or countenance he communicated that little truth she wanted to know. It may be that he knew that she knew he had done so; or that he knew she already knew her little truth.

But, except for these possibilities, it must be recorded to my great astonishment that Lehmann *writes* that he avoided her question and *changed the subject*. He said, '. . . when in the next days and weeks the going gets hard, remember you are not alone! Jesus Christ . . .'[3] Thus, he brought up the Truth when the truth was asked. He spoke of the 'truth situation' all Christians know they are in, of the ultimates of the Christian context. Certainly not with the same intentionality as Pilate who, hard pressed as he was with the burdens of wading through, turned from the small question about justice and truth in his official acts to open the great question, 'What is the Truth?' To Pilate's question Lehmann had a positive answer, and of this he spoke quietly with his friend. That was, of course, the most important thing to speak of in that hour, or at any hour! However, on the supposition that Lehmann left her little question unanswered (and did not answer it non-verbally) as he turned to the most important matter, it would seem that he (if he was the one to tell her) withheld the truth from someone to whom that truth belonged—that little truth as well as Christ the Truth. That *respect*, that truth, he still owed her in

[1] p. 133. [2] pp. 132-3 (italics added). [3] p. 133.

CE F   73

her mortality; and he ought not to have treated her dying as something to which she was merely *patient*, something to be passed over. She was the (small letter) *subject* of that dying and the honour owed her, in this regard also, ought not to have been avoided in their common devotion to *the* Subject of all Christian living and dying.

Nothing of present moment depends upon the correctness of this opinion of mine concerning the bearing of Truth-telling upon truth-telling. The point is that Lehmann has not undertaken to tell us what he thinks concerning this question, unless changing the subject is his answer to it. Therefore Truth-telling goes on above the situations, the hospital rooms, courts and market-places in which (small letter) truths must be told, and it has no stated or proven relevance to them. One wonders whether that justice and truth was so 'non-preceptual' which the Hebrew prophets urged should be done 'in the gate' and throughout all the relations among men.[1]

2. *Koinonia and porneia*[2]

Again we are placed on notice by the author that the 'ethical meaning and guidance' provided for sexual behaviour when it is set within the 'liberating and humanising context' of the *koinonia* cannot be fully set forth in a volume on the 'methodology' of Christian ethics, but 'belongs properly to the substance or content of Christian ethics'—to follow.[3] Still sexual ethics, not itself random, seems to be more than a 'random instance of contextual behaviour'[4]; and what is said on this subject in the present volume does not fail to enter upon the substance and the content of Christian ethics which, in the author's opinion, properly follows from adopting his methodology.

Lehmann's remarks about sex ethics are laudably motivated by the aim of avoiding a morality of venereal fears and tabus or a morality of venereal frivolity. He wants to avoid libidinal

[1] The foregoing is reprinted, with permission of the Editor, from *Theology Today*, January 1965.
[2] I use this sub-section title just for the fun of it. It is evident that *porneia* has already been ruled out. (See John A. T. Robinson, *Christian Morals Today*, p. 32, for a discussion of the meaning of this term.) My title should, however, draw attention to the fact and make it evident that an act-*koinonia* ethics establishes itself as an ethic without principles or rules or virtues by omitting to begin at the beginning with the precepts it certifies.
[3] p. 139.   [4] p. 132.

sexual repression without falling into the encouragement of enlightened libidinal indulgence with their distortions of the human spirit.[1] In fact in this connexion Lehmann makes what is for him a remarkably preceptual statement, nay, even a proscriptive statement, to the effect that in a Christian context promiscuous sexual acts (and not only prostitution) 'simply have no place. They are *ab initio* sexual deviations.'[2] From this not insignificant beginning, a fuller articulation of Christian sex ethics might be expected. This will be forthcoming provided the author sets some of his other thoughts in order, and if in particular he follows out the methodological consequences of the fact that he has just allowed that from *the ethical* in a wholly non-preceptual sense, from an ethics of 'freedom in obedience', unqualified ethical imperatives, even if secondary ones, can somehow be derived. I shall not inquire into the consistency between the judgment that promiscuity, which is all over the place, has no place and the declaration that a Christian ethics can be written which permits no gap to open up between the ethical claim and the ethical act.

The important thing to note about Lehmann's treatment of sex ethics, however, is the fact that he accepts the most egregious error thoughtlessly propounded by the modern world 'come of age' concerning the traditional Christian teachings in regard to marriage. He identifies the traditional theology of marriage with a theology of the marriage *ceremony*. In all but one instance of his use of the word 'marriage', it means the ceremony or the legalities in the sphere of church or state. It must be said that *that* was never the church's teaching about sex and marriage, at least never before the bourgeois period (and not rightly even then). The bourgeois period did develop an ethics of social respectability as its highest norm for the sexual relation, along with its notion of absolute property right, which in turn helped to corrupt the traditional meaning of the marriage covenant to mean placing on record an exchange of absolute and exclusive rights of sexual dominion. Against this the present age has rebelled with its notion of marriage as 'contract'.[3] In any case, a bourgeois theology of the marriage ceremony shapes Lehmann's understanding of the traditional

---

[1] p. 136.   [2] p. 138.
[3] cf. my article 'Marriage Law and Biblical Covenant', in *Religion and the Public Order*, ed. by D. Giannella. The University of Chicago Press, 1964, pp. 41-77.

75

teaching. It also shapes, and misshapes, his understanding of a sex ethics of 'freedom in obedience' which will set sexual behaviour in 'a liberating and humanising context', not simply in the context of the ceremony (which Lehmann mistakenly calls 'marriage').

The tradition of Christian ethics, Lehmann writes, 'regarded marriage as the legitimisation of the sexual act'. It 'exalted marriage as the norm of sexual permissiveness'. It enforced 'the marriage criterion', and insisted on 'conformity'.[1]

In contrast, Lehmann wants 'the sexual act . . . loosed from the marriage criterion'. This makes eminent sense if by 'marriage' Lehmann means the ceremony. It makes almost none at all if he does not. For the sentence just quoted continues with the proposal that the sexual act be 'anchored in the human reality of encounter between male and female under conditions of trust and fulfilment which such an encounter both nourishes and presupposes'.[2] Take away the occasionalism that creeps in through the word 'encounter' (and which has already been proscribed by the precept against promiscuity) and, of course, take away the assumption that what God is characteristically doing in the world to effectuate His purposes for the humanisation of men and women is to act literally by the 'moment', 'day' or 'year' in which they should follow Him. Take away that, I say, and Lehmann's statement comes close to affirming what the church has always meant by marriage.

In this interpretation of Lehmann, I confess that I have imposed a meaning upon the word 'marriage' as he uses it, which remains obscure. It is, however, the least pejorative interpretation, since the alternative to assigning a legal and ceremonial meaning to 'marriage' is to say that he has simply begged the question about (in lieu of a ceremony) what ought to be the meaning of that 'openness' and consent to the being of one's partner, that 'trust' and (marital?) 'belonging' which in a Christian context should precede or accompany the sex act for this to be a fully responsible act.

The meaning of this is what should be articulated and debated among theological ethicists today in living dialogue with all that was ever said by the tradition about marriage and its perdurance as an ordinance made for man. Instead,

[1] p. 136. [2] p. 137.

Lehmann joins the present age in its feckless debate with a bourgeois theology of the marriage ceremony now no longer effectual among us, and which was never the church's meaning when it understood covenant-consent and covenant-responsibility to be the humanising context of the sex act.

Lehmann struggles to free himself from such a degraded legalistic notion of marriage. His first formulation is: *'It is not marriage which legitimises the sexual act but the sexual act which legitimises marriage.'* But the word 'legitimises' (rightly connected as it is with the legalistic meaning of 'marriage' in the first part of that sentence) does not seem to him quite apt for what he wants to affirm in the latter part. So he tries again, and writes: *'It is not marriage which fulfils the sexual act but the sexual act which fulfils marriage.'*[1] Here is perhaps one instance in which the word 'marriage' takes on more than ceremonial or legalistic meaning: *marriage* does this, and not simply the trusting sex act, and in the sequence and connexion exhibited in the assertion: it is 'the sexual act which fulfils marriage'. So always said the tradition. What does Lehmann think consummation means?

But Lehmann is not yet quite free in his apprehension of marriage as a relationship that is before and deeper than any ceremony and therefore fit to be before the sex act as its humanising context which is then 'fulfilled' by the conjugal act. The limitations of this formulation is most evident in what it leads Lehmann, in the first part of the statement, to attribute to the tradition in order to make it fit for rejection. No instructed Christian theologian of the past would have said that 'marriage fulfils the sexual act', since this would mean that marriage is made by copulation and comes only as its completion (which rather seems to be the modern view). The tradition would no more have said that 'marriage fulfills the sexual act'—in any sense of the word 'fulfills'—than Lehmann can feel comfortable about saying in his first attempted reversal, that it is the sexual act which legitimises marriage.

In any case, to speak of 'a complete and transforming partnership which can be neither complete nor transforming apart from what can be finely called "the communion of the body"'[2] is not the radical reversal of traditional teachings *in regard to the marriage relation* which Lehmann imagines it to be,

[1] p. 137.   [2] p. 137.

77

though it does suggest a radical improvement of ancient views about sexuality as among the 'goods' of marriage.

Of course, Lehmann's approximation to the traditional understanding of the marriage relation is deficient. This is a fruit of his ceaseless polemic against an understanding of marriage that tradition never meant. This prevents him from making a significant contribution to a further understanding of this subject even by way of important corrections of the understanding of *marriage* which prevailed in former ages.

Instead, Lehmann, having approached the borders of 'a complete and transforming partnership' does not continue with an exploration of that, but instead falls back into accenting (against marriage believed to be among the legalities) the fact that 'such an ethic can offer no sexual guidance according to a blue print to apply to all sexual behaviour in the same way'.[1] He boldly includes 'the sexual act among the risks of free obedience',[2] which of course it is. But that tells us little about the Christian meaning of free obedience, or obedient freedom, or the implications of this for marriage. Lehmann, however, 'hopes' that his 'axiom of reversal' (which we have seen to be no reversal) will lead 'toward a heightening rather than a weakening of the integrity of the sexual relation and of fidelity in marriage'.[3]

Thus he wants to have his Christian fidelity and also wants to play to the ear of the groundlings of the present age. Each of these concerns brunts the other. He wants 'sexual intensity . . . creatively related to sexual sensitivity' without coming clear about what that means or to what it should lead. Or again, he writes about sexual experience 'intrinsic to human wholeness in and through human belonging', and then immediately precludes an openminded exploration of what 'belonging' may and can and should mean, by adding: 'whether the sexual act occurs within the marriage relationship or on the way toward marriage'.[4] Apparently these are equal alternatives for the free, sensitive and obedient human heart; and that, of course, is *the* ethical question to which Lehmann presupposes an answer, or undertakes to give none. The tradition was much wiser in its ability to take into account sexual acts on the way to marriage without making a 'principle' of it.

[1] p. 137.   [2] p. 138.   [3] p. 139.   [4] p. 138.

Moreover, Lehmann must simply be informed that it is later than he thinks in the social history of contextualism, and therefore too late for Christian contextualism to imagine that it is saying anything important by speaking of 'sexual acts on the way to marriage' in either a bourgeois or a Christian sense, with no attempt to explicate the full Christian meaning of marriage which sexual behaviour is supposed to be on its way toward. It is too late for this Christian contextualism because it is necessarily dependent upon the structural concepts to be supplied by and articulated in a Christian *ethos* and upon the silent assumptions of an age which give Christian meaning to such words as 'belonging' or to 'wholeness' or integrity in marriage. The ethos and the assumptions are no longer there to place sexual behaviour upon any particular route. The relevant sounding words about relating 'the sexual act to human belonging' and 'human belonging to marriage' actually are today suspended in mid-air. In this book, they express a *programme* not seriously undertaken.

We are forced to conclude that Christian contextualism does not develop a positive account of norms because it secretly depends on them, and expects a Christian *ethos* to supply a moral context which it no longer is there to give. Lehmann's contextualism is decades too late.

For Lehmann to undertake to *set* sexual acts on the way to *marriage* (in any other sense than the arrangement, alongside 'responsible' love, for breeding and educating children to which the current 'sexual revolution' has reduced it whilst ignorantly accusing the tradition of exactly that) will bring him into productive dialogue with traditional Christian teachings and into conflict with the present age with in particular its misunderstanding of that tradition. It will also bring him in touch with more elements and ethical implications of *the Christian context* than the single reference in which he places the 'encounter' between a man and a woman into 'encounter with him who reigns in forgiveness and renewal over human failure and defeat'.[1] It will bring him into touch also with Ephesians 5 which determines and nourishes the Christian ethical (not necessarily sacramental) meaning of marriage by reference to Christ's inseverable love for the church as criterion. This is 'the marriage criterion'. This precludes specialising in the

[1] p. 139.

exception, to which the divine forgiveness and renewal after human failure are most directly pertinent when these are left standing alone. In fact, without other Christian teachings in regard to marriage the word 'failure' has no meaning given it by reference to Christ, and there remain only sexual acts along many ways in quest of wholeness.

3. *The justifiedness of Christian participation in war*

Here pacifism is the 'absolutist' position Lehmann takes as the foil to show that a prescriptive approach is not 'really consonant with a Christian ethic'. There was, of course, a gap between the pacifist ethical claim and acts of war; and in the midst of war a turmoil, perhaps an unnecessary turmoil, was brought about in the consciences of Christian pacifists because of a 'conflict between what they believed to be Christian teaching and what they found themselves unable to avoid'.[1] But this introduction to the problem has to be set entirely aside as not necessarily pointing to the virtues of a contextual ethic. It may only be that 'what they believed to be Christian teaching, was in error.'

It is in connexion with the morality of Christian participation in war, however, that Lehmann waxes most contextual and utters most brilliantly his theological absolutes in asserted relevance to an ethical problem. It is here that he asserts that 'there is never any one way as against all others for dealing with any human situation', and here he brings in God's imagination. Here again he reiterates that *koinonia* ethics is 'never a matter of having really done *the good*' (italics added); it is rather a matter of having really 'been on the track of God's doing'. I should not have said 'really', for getting on the track of God's doing is as difficult as doing the good. So we must say it is never a matter of 'having really' done either. *Koinonia* life in time of war (or peace) is 'bracketed by the dynamics of God's political activity on the one hand and God's forgiveness on the other'.[2]

All this is theology and I will not presume to assess whether it is a good or sufficient statement of Christian theology. But it is not ethics, even if these are wholly valid perspectives and however much they may have *indirectly* to do with ethics. The moral response required and made possible in wartime by this

[1] p. 140. [2] p. 141.

understanding of the Christian context is simply 'taking in trust the risk of trust'.[1] But that is not ethics either, however much more ultimate and important it may be. It is rather a religious attitude appropriate to all our works, from which of course important consequences may flow for the moral life. To take in trust the risk of trust is relevant to all choices; it has therefore little or no light to shed upon any particular choice or upon the *problem* of *choice* itself. It does not tell us how to get on the track (or do the good), but only sustains our trust and hope that we are, or, if not, God is.

Lehmann next writes, as he must, that 'such an ethic' will sound 'puzzling, even ridiculous' to anyone who has not the 'eyes to see the signs of the times'. In face of this appeal to the hiddenness of the *koinonia* behind the eyes of faith and to the hiddenness of 'the times' or of the track God is on behind the choices before us in actual politics, it becomes difficult to remember that a strength of this whole approach to Christian ethics is said to be its relevance. And in face of the gap here that is far greater than any between ethical claim and act, it is impossible even to understand that ethics was said to have now become a *descriptive* discipline[2] and not an imperative one.

Lehmann not only makes this 'ridiculous' point. He insists upon it, and proves it by the fact that 'even so sophisticated a daily as *The New York Times*' could not understand what the theologians were saying in the 1950 report on *The Christian Conscience and Weapons of Mass Destruction*. What the theologians communicated to journalists and other intelligent people in the actual world of political choices was clear enough[3]; but what, according to Lehmann, the journalists should have received and what the theologians intended to say was utterly ambiguous. No journalist can be expected to understand that, not because of the nature of journalists but because of the nature of ambiguity!

In Lehmann's view, what the Federal Council of Churches document declared was actually an ambiguous 'Yes' and 'No'. It declared that 'war is *never* a Christian possibility and on the other hand that war is *always* a possibility which a Christian

[1] p. 141.   [2] p. 14.
[3] The *N.Y. Times* got the point very well indeed, when to the headline 'Church Unit Backs Use of Atom Bomb' is added (as any newspaper reader knows to be proper form) the sub-headline: 'Nuclear Attack on U.S. or Allies Made Condition of Sanction' (28th November 1950).

may not be able ultimately to avoid'.[1] Was this double-talk? No, says Lehmann. 'A *koinonia* ethic would insist' the FCC 'was not engaged in double-talk but in speaking the right or living word.'[2]

This requires explication. It means that 'war is ethically ambiguous'—with which no one, I suppose, disagrees. But then the ambiguity is explained to mean that 'war *both* contradicts what God is doing in the world to bring about a new humanity and is instrumental to this activity'.[3] Since Lehmann cannot be making generalisations about war in general, but is thinking contextually (as did the document in question) about a particular action of war under given circumstances, our journalist may be excused from seeing how a particular act of war can at the same time be both contradictory to and instrumental to what God is doing. Perhaps there is some profound religious meaning in these assertions, he might dimly apprehend, hidden in God's inscrutable rulership upon which it is significant for human life to be oriented through an acknowledgment that His purposes overarch the whole of man's political decisions and destiny. But the document and Christian ethics and church political pronouncements will seem to him designed to go the point of clarifying what a nation or a Christian should do or not do in politics when there are options for choice before us.

Lost in the desert of ambiguity, a man may well yearn for 'the irrelevance of ethical absolutism' or else yield to 'the expediency of ethical relativism' instead of finding the way to overcome these 'dismal alternatives'.[4] A man will want to know what *thrust* to make with his life when he takes 'in trust the risk of trust'.[5] Acknowledging that he cannot make his actions *right*, and that their *rightness* depends on their potential instrumentality within God's purposes, he will still want to know, if he can do anything, what can make one decision rather than another somewhat more '*potentially instrumental* to the divine activity in the world'. To this question, which is the Christian ethical question, it helps not at all to say that 'the freedom of the divine initiative cannot be abrogated by any human decision'; or for a man to be told that it is 'a matter of the Christian's *hope*' whether and how far his actions 'actually

---

[1] p. 142. [2] p. 142. [3] p. 143 (italics added).
[4] p. 143. [5] p. 141.

82

served the purposes of God in fashioning a new humanity'.[1] All this is true and profound and important, but it is neither relevant nor expedient nor Christian enough to be all there is to the living word that needs to be spoken in politics.

While emphasising that 'the ethical originality of Christianity lies in its refusal to ignore or to weaken ambiguity', however, Lehmann does not fail to indicate 'the considerations which make such decisions possible'.[2] In so far as these considerations are references to the ultimate context of all human action, they tell us how uninstructed 'decisions in obedience' may be expected and religiously sustained in the midst of ambiguity. In so far, however, as these are considerations of a Christian ethical order, they do provide some direction for choice and action. They tell us something about the *thrust* of trust in politics.

In his discussion of *The Christian Conscience and Weapons of Mass Destruction*, I find two such considerations or thrusts. (1) In support of that document's defence of U.S. responsibility to mount a nuclear deterrent and use or at least threaten to use it in response to an attack upon our allies or ourselves, Lehmann writes: 'American Christians . . . could not live out their lives in this world in disregard of fellow Christians and fellow human beings in other parts of the world.'[3] Lest we forsake our neighbours and leave them defenceless, there could be no 'categorical prohibition of the use of nuclear weapons'.[4] This is a love-derived justification of U.S. responsibility for massive deterrence (perhaps for an actual second strike—though Lehmann does not go into being ambiguous about *that*). (2) '*It is plain*', Lehmann writes, 'that the love of neighbour as a principle of action derived from the love of God excludes acts which *initiate* war or lead to war.'[5]

That is a correct statement, under the first point, of the source and meaning of the justifiedness of Christian responsibility in military decisions. Moreover, if 'American Christians could not live out their lives in this world in disregard of fellow Christians and fellow human beings in other parts of the world', it is *not at all plain* that they should make a categorical prohibition of this nation's positive or first use of its power, in interventions or other acts that may *initiate* war. Lehmann says

[1] p. 144 (first italics added).   [2] p. 144.   [3] pp. 142-3.
[4] p. 143.   [5] p. 143 (italics added).

the right thing under the first point, but not enough of critical import about what a Christian should ever do; and he says too much in his second about what a Christian should never do.

Thus, in so far as this *koinonia* ethics does not dwell in ambiguity, the twin implications to be found in it for the guidance of Christian political action in regard to participation in war turn out to be precisely those contained in the American ethos which came to fill the vacuum. This is the American aggressor-defender doctrine of the 'just war', the final product of which was our massive deterrence military policy coupled with an immobilised foreign policy. No considerations are articulated which govern what should be done in defence, no morality of war; and no considerations would seem ever to justify war's start. Prior to war's occasion in unjustified aggression, nothing stirs Chistian responsibility so far as the use of force is concerned; after war's start, there are only technical problems to be solved and no moral issues about what should be done in war, or in deterrence.

Lehmann's 'Yes' is too unqualified on his first point and his 'No' is too emphatic on the second. This happens when the 'Yes-No' of ambiguous obedience in faith is unlocked: without further ethical reflection, one has no protection against saying 'Yes' or 'No' whenever common opinion says 'Yes' or 'No' and in its manner. Are we called in such wise to take in trust the risk of trust that our decisions and actions may still by God's grace be found potentially instrumental to His activity in the world? The traditional just war doctrine, to which Lehmann has refused to listen, did better than that on both points.

Lehmann repeats the canard[1] that traditional Christian teachings about the 'just war' are a peculiar Roman Catholic possession and that its criteria are supposed to entail 'precise distinctions' between events and situations in history.[2] Yet in 1961 I tried to demonstrate that in essential respects this theory came to birth in Christian moral reflection because of the pressures of and the refinements required by Christian love-in-action.[3] In so far as Lehmann articulates considerations that

[1] My dictionary defines this word to mean 'an extravagant or absurd report or story set afloat to delude the public'.
[2] p. 142.
[3] See my *War and the Christian Conscience*. Durham, N.C.: The Duke University Press, 1961, ch. 3. This chapter examines, in fact, a prime example of rule-agapism in the history of Christian ethics.

provide minimum guidance for political action, these too are suggestions about the meaning of responsible action in war-time that are the requirements of Christian love for neighbour. That is Lehmann's language too. It can be affirmed that the teachings about the just war in their recurrence in Christian conscience and their continuity through time was a product of the *agapé* meaning of *koinonia* ethics almost from its beginning until now. This is the oldest *koinonia* ethics on the subject of the justifiedness of Christian participation in the uses of power. A sign of this is the fact that this matter was always discussed by theologians in all ages under the treatise on charity. How-ever much the expression 'just war' may be an inadequate one, or even offensive, and however much no Christian today should be rigidly bound by the conclusions of the past, the task is to try to see with the eyes of faith and love at least as deeply into what is entailed in Christian ethics itself for and into contem-porary political realities. This task can only be avoided by setting the just war theory outside the *koinonia* (which, aside from its consequence in denying to ourselves a source for the sensitising and instruction of our consciences, is simply a gross error in the historical and systematic interpretation of Christian ethics).

Observe what happens when Lehmann makes too fresh a beginning in *koinonia* ethics, or when he does not persevere in the articulation, the questioning and correction of the con-siderations he begins to set forth. Just as before he substituted Truth-telling for truth-telling, so now he substitutes Recon-ciliation at the moment of decision in question for the work of graceful reason and love-in-action seeking to determine and do 'justice' in actual concrete political choices.

This is the upshot of his discussion of Hiroshima and Nagasaki. Lehmann asks: 'What were the ethical considerations involved in the judgment and the action taken *at that time*?'[1] The *intention* was to end the war and to save lives. If these good intentions and a concern for consequences was all that was involved at that time in the decision, or culpably absent from it, then of course Lehmann is correct in his observation that 'the destructive consequences of the use of nuclear weapons could not be limited by the normative judgment in terms of which the decision was taken'. He concludes from this: 'Here

[1] p. 241.

was a conspicuous exception to a conspicuous ethical norm', namely, that 'human life is a good which must be safe-guarded rather than destroyed'.[1] Why this was a 'conspicuous exception' is not clear, if these terms are an adequate analysis of the decision-making process at the time, since I suppose the risk of trust was taken in trust and with some reasonable calculation that more lives would be saved by dropping the bomb than by fighting on the beaches of Japan. The bombs that fell over these cities were in no sense 'exceptions to the logic of ethical generalisation',[2] but cases of it, the generalisations being limited to determining the actions that should be chosen because of their conduciveness to choiceworthy consequences.

In any case, there was more involved in the decision at that time. President Truman said not only 'Save the greater number lives' but also 'Drop it on a *military* target', i.e. *an open city*. Robert Batchelder[3] has shown that the option of dropping it on a large military installation was *not even considered* as an alternative, just as earlier the destruction of Japan's intricate system of railroads was not considered as a target possibly to be preferred over using our bombers to set fire to Tokyo night after night. The very meaning of *legitimate* military objectives had been completely eroded from the minds of men during the course of the war. *That* was a factor decisive at the time the decision was made, *missing* from it.

Lehmann gives himself this 'conspicuous exception' to ethical norms by, first, forgetting that the logic of ethical generalisation from the norm of saving rather than destroying human life requires and is not at all contradicted by an act that it is believed will save more while destroying many lives; and, second, by passing over the conspicuous absence *at the time* of ethical norms governing warfare that had been the fruit of the most ancient and widely held *koinonia* ethics of them all, namely, the just war theory. He would have had to go into that, or something like it of the same order of political relevance, in order to speak the truth about or to that situation.

Instead he speaks the Truth. He seeks to find in Hiroshima and Nagasaki evidence for reading the situation *at that time* as a 'transvaluational exception' in which 'Christianity specialises'.

---

[1] p. 242.   [2] p. 242.
[3] *The Irreversible Decision* 1939-1950. Boston, Mass.: Houghton Mifflin Co., 1962.

He even seems to compare these events, or what God was (*sic*) doing in them, with the man healed on the Sabbath day, the woman taken in adultery, the good Samaritan and the prodigal son as all vivid instances of 'an exception that suspends the rule' and 'challenges previously accepted ethical judgments and patterns of behaviour and breaks fresh ethical ground'.[1] Actually the ingredient missing from the decision to drop the bombs was any memory of what was implied in precisely these transvaluational exceptions in Jesus' teaching for man's concrete political and military conduct.

Lehmann continues to *assert* that there was '*at that time*, another possibility which is still an ethical option'—and not only that there was *at that time* ethical ambiguity concerning what to do at Hiroshima.[2] Yet this is plainly retrospective interpretation of what God *was* doing in the world, overruling man's evil, and of course is still doing in the age inaugurated by the first and last use of atomic power as an instrument of war. He finds in the devastation of these cities 'signs of God's pressure toward a global implementation of the full humanity of man' and declares their destruction 'to that extent ethically significant and defensible'.[3] Now, one can perhaps say that God may do or permit evil that good may come of it. He can certainly say that God overrules the good and evil actions of men so that good comes of it. But one ought not to say that now, at this time, a proper response to what God *is* doing in the world is that we should do evil (or do ambiguity where it is possible to come to greater clarity) in order that He may bring good out of it. Only retrospectively, when reflecting on what we now can see God *was* doing, is it proper to see in such events the ethical significance that from them God has brought forth a new possibility and need for the global implementation of the full humanity of man.

Lehmann actually has no more to say that could have been said or done at that time than U.S. policy said and did. He fills in the gap by reference to the 'transvaluation' of all the norms we violated which God *was* doing in the world. True, he *says* that there was another possibility *at that time*: the particular convergences upon that 'single moment of decision *could have been* ethically understood and explained as requiring and action which moved the concrete human situation to a

[1] p. 243.   [2] p. 244.   [3] p. 244.

new level of freedom, power, and order'.[1] Surely he is here reading a possibility back into that situation. The army among the Japanese services *wanted* to fight on the beaches, and they almost succeeded in assassinating the Emperor when after Hiroshima he unconstitutionally intervened to begin to bring the war to an end. Lehmann cannot possibly be taken seriously to mean as an ethical and political judgment that the bearing of Truth upon truth, of Reconciliation upon political choices, could have produced at that time and in that moment a new political ordering of mankind. Yet this is what he says, in order to make a Christian contextualism devoid of any structural elements of ethical or political reflection (i.e. devoid of any examination of the morality of war itself) seem relevant to the situation. That this was a quite impossible possibility is as much as admitted: 'the existing political sovereignties and structures *were incommensurate and unprepared*' for the 'bold re-examination of the ethical foundation and use of power' which was 'required'.[2] So what God *is* doing in the world goes on over the heads of men and nations; and from insight into this Christians seem unable to say more about political decisions in wartime than the nations do. The gap here between *the ethical reality* (as Lehmann prefers to call it) and the choices for action open for men is far greater than in any so-called preceptual ethics.

It may be true, of course, that the bold venture required of mankind in the nuclear age cannot be ventured without crossing the boundary from ethics and politics into religion. But as the proposal of an option for the warring nations *at that time* this would have required crossing the boundary again from religion into political miracle. Of course, it is *now* possible to see that what God *was* doing at Hiroshima and still is doing in His politics is to require of mankind a thorough-going revision of the uses and institutions of power. But then this will still mean an application of the *agapé* and *koinonia* ethics enshrined in the principles governing the just uses of power. For the global domestication of force, it can be demonstrated, requires the legalisation or institutional ordering of world politics in accord with the principles of the just war theory. That body of teachings only states the bearing of Reconciliation upon reconciliation among men in so far as this requires that the force

[1] p. 244.   [2] p. 243 (italics added).

which must be used to preserve human life and tolerable community be surrounded by specifiable limits upon its exercise. Perhaps mankind will one day make this response to what God is doing in the world. But a Christian ethics which does not know enough to say more than this contextualism about Hiroshima *at the time* is not apt to prove able to fulfil its responsibility towards the present and future life of mankind by articulating from the interior of its religious insights the ingredients of a political ethic for *this* time A. H. (after Hiroshima). Thus alone can 'reconciliation become a political reality'.[1]

A not insignificant point may be added to the above. Just as Lehmann understands the decision at Hiroshima to be one of inward intention oriented upon the end of saving lives (and not also one misshapen exteriorly by the absence of any limits upon conduct or means), so also he understands Roman Catholic moral theology to be primarily concerned about the intention (and not beyond this also concerned with the shape of actual conduct) in a principal feature that is of importance in the traditional Christian morality in regard to the conduct of war. He explains one of their theologians to mean, in what he wrote about intending the good effect and not the evil effect of an action, that the good effects intended justify putting forth the action not only in the face of foreseeable evil consequences, but also in the face of avoidable evil consequences, and, it seems, without shaping the actions so as to avoid these consequences if they can be avoided. 'If an action ought to have been pursued' because of the good intended, he writes, 'even though the evil effects of the action could have been foreseen, and could (*sic*) have been prevented, the action is good and not evil.'[2] The truth is that the word 'not' should be inserted in that sentence where my 'sic' is. I am ready to believe this a typographical error rather than to believe Lehmann mistaken, except for the fact that the same crucial omission occurs five lines above this one.

Christian love shaped itself for action, and it shaped *action* and not the intention alone, in surrounding non-combatants with moral immunity from *direct* attack. This does not simply mean from intended attack. The foreseen evil effect that was allowed was always understood to be an *unavoidable* one. No

[1] p. 244.
[2] p. 293.

amount of good intention justified doing avoidable evil. Reinhold Niebuhr is in agreement with this celebrated rule of 'double effect' when in his 'responsibilist' ethic he includes within the meaning of political and military responsibility a course of action which chooses the greater good in the midst of also doing a lesser evil. Only he says this not so exactly, and his language is different. Niebuhr says 'it is responsible' where the Catholic moralist says, 'it is permitted' to adopt a course of action which can achieve a greater good (or a lesser evil than the one prevented) even when there are also comparatively lesser evils unavoidably consequent upon this same course of action. Both positions result from Christian love-in-action, and shaping action, on the part of persons who, as Lehmann wrote, 'could not live out their lives in this world in disregard of their fellow human beings'[1] even though to live in this world means to be engaged in action that always unavoidably has multiple good and evil consequences.

It was pointed out that in his 'special ethics' Karl Barth surrounds and locates an 'exception' which is then steadfastly preserved in its nature as an exception (or as an instance of application) by its environment in Christian ethical understanding into what God is doing in the world to make and keep human life human. It was also pointed out that Barth's 'exception' continues to bear the burden placed upon it by knowledge of the claim God has placed on human life in the matter to which exception is called for in a complete ethics of freedom in obedience. In conclusion, I might point out that a great many (though not all) of Barth's 'exceptions' for choice are susceptible of illumination or 'solution' in terms of the so-called rule of double effect, which is only an extension of the analysis of right Christian conduct in terms of love-in-action and love-shaping-action (and not only or mainly an application of 'natural justice'). Barth's exceptions fall within his discussion of 'respect for life', 'the protection of life', etc.; and here he finds some very hard choices some of which involve the conflict of life with life. It was precisely in the midst of thinking about such situations that traditional Christian ethics and Roman Catholic moral theology extended the requirements of obedient love into the concrete contexts and difficult decisions of men one step beyond the point to which this expressly

[1] pp. 142-3.

90

brought Barth.[1] This is to say, Roman Catholic moral theology would *in principle* surround and locate the exceptional choice that may be uniquely obedient to God's claim one step removed from where Barth came upon this. The forbidden self-destruction and the prohibited murder are *defined* as *direct* killing. *Theoretically*, there may still be cases that fall outside this refinement of how a Christian can and may and must serve life. It would therefore *in principle* be possible to say of exceptions to the *agapé* and *koinonia*-shaped 'rule of double effect', or to say of decisions that fall outside the guidance this supplies for conscience, all the great things Barth says about exceptional obedience under the call and permission of God. It is only that Roman Catholic moral theologians discover no such exceptional cases in which sovereign charity should prevail in freely determining the good to be done apart from the direction of life by divine charity in the past in the thinking of the *koinonia* about these matters. In this they are mistaken.

It will indeed be an anomaly if Lehmann's *koinonia* ethics become the mind of the Protestant churches in this age, and if our thinking about Christian ethics assumed a shape that is much further removed than is Barth's from fruitful dialogue with the Christian ethics that is done in the Roman Catholic tradition. For this is an era in which it is widely supposed that there is something to be gained from a re-examination of the Protestant tradition and, by doing so and in doing so, from an ecumenical dialogue with Roman Catholicism at the supersonic (and doubtless more important) levels of our respective and possibly common understanding of church, tradition and theology. Is this to be programmatically ruled out in the realm of ethics?

One might quarrel with Paul Lehmann about whether 'the clarification of ethical principles . . . is a *logical* enterprise'. He might ask who ever believed that there is a way '*in logic* of closing the gap between the abstract and the concrete'?[2] Certainly not the 'expendable' natural law with its emphasis on the need for practical wisdom. And one might ask whether precisely the error of the 'middle axiom' people was not that they agreed with Lehmann that there should be a way *in logic*

---

[1] See however *C-D*, III/4, pp. 425 and 427, for points at which Barth's thinking about the service of life in cases of the conflict of life with life is itself forced to distinguish between direct and indirect killing and thus to begin to take the shape of service in accord with the love-inspired rule of double effect.

[2] p. 152 (italics added).

91

of closing the gap between ethical claims and ethical action.

But all that would be of secondary importance, however instructive it might prove to the author. Far more important it is to point out the far, far greater gap in Lehmann's system of ethics between the Christian context and any actual context, bridged as this is by very little ethical clarification; and to call attention to the alternative ways in which this gap must necessarily disguise itself. Far more important it is to point out what happens when ethics in a Christian context is properly defined as 'being what it has been given me to be', being and doing what I am 'in the context of the Truth'[1] without an enormous amount of solid clarifying Christian ethical reflection about what this means for the direction of action. Without this, Christian contextualism swings high above the social context, or else unsorted-out elements of the secular context are elevated into identification with it. Doing the Truth becomes without more ado the only truth to be done and so the Christian context is really irrelevant to actual behaviour, or else what is being done or something in the secular context, whether its ideals or its actuality, is absolutised and becomes the Truth. One might venture to predict, for example, what 'organic interrelational differentiation'[2] will produce when that is taken as a clue to what God is doing in the world in the matter of racial integration. Will this not be a highly relevant-sounding instance of postulating 'at the same time the free expression of the individual and . . . absolute social cohesion', which J. L. Talmon[3] defined as the nature of all utopianism?

Doubtless 'the indicative character of the Christian ethos . . . underlies every ethical imperative'. Doubtless this 'underlines the provisional character of such imperatives.' And doubtless it 'ultimately suspends them',[4] because God is merciful. But to fail to underline the imperatives, to underline their provisional character too heavily, or to presume to suspend them too quickly ourselves, raises no question more certainly than whether there is any light to our feet or guide along the pathways of life. It raises no question more certainly than the question whether there is any such thing as Christian ethics, or only religious solace for the absence of it.

[1] p. 159.   [2] p. 66.
[3] *Utopianism and Politics*, p. 13.   [4] cf. p. 161.

92

V

AN UNFINISHED AGENDA

IN a recent essay on 'Love and Principle in Christian Ethics'[1] Professor William K. Frankena continues to chide the theologians for failing to say clearly what they mean by Christian normative ethics. He believes that 'its theological proponents may be selling Christian ethics short by their manner of expounding and defending it'.[2] A philosopher, he writes, reading in the literature of Christian ethics, 'is bound to be struck, not only by the topics discussed and the claims made, but by the relative absence of careful definition, clear statement, or cogent and rigorous argument, as these are judged by the standards with which he is familiar in his own field (even if he does not himself always conform to them)'.[3] Frankena wants to do something toward remedying the situation. He proposes to do this by again indicating positions 'that are possible'.[4] With a number of wry comments about his own proclivity for multiplying categories and upon the fact that like all mankind he 'has sought out many inventions',[5] he proposes a dozen or more types when you take account of the combinations that are possible.

Thus, this essay contains a fuller delineation of the options in Christian ethical theory than those he began to set forth in his book on *Ethics*, with which I launched the present analysis of doing Christian ethics. Again, I believe that Frankena's types may prove helpful if these are brought into consideration; and in particular that a somewhat simplified review of his suggestions may assist us in identifying or projecting an unfinished agenda for Christian normative ethics.[6]

The following, according to Frankena, are the several distinguishable types that are possible or actual.

---

[1] In *Faith and Philosophy* (ed. by Alvin Plantinga). Grand Rapids, Michigan: Wm. B. Eerdmans Publishing Co., 1964. It will be unfortunate if, because it was published in a *Festschrift*, this essay does not receive the attention it deserves.

[2] p. 204.   [3] p. 203.

[4] p. 204.   [5] p. 219.

[6] In contrast to the analysis of particular moral or social problems, on the one hand, or, on the other, Christian meta-ethics, which searches out the justification of the principle or principles of normative ethics.

1. *Pure Agapism*

This general position 'assigns to the "law of love" the same position that utilitarianism assigns to the principle of utility; it allows no *basic* ethical principles other than or independent of "the law of love"'.[1] In order that the point of Frankena's suggestions for the doing of constructive Christian ethics be not blunted, it should be noted that his typology sits loose within the terminology he employs, and would be repeated if a Christian ethicist judges that it is better to use some other root word in place of *agapé*. Someone may object to using love as the 'primitive idea' in Christian ethics; or someone may object to calling love a 'principle'. To them Frankena replies: '. . . What interests me here is not so much the question whether love or the love-command is itself a rule or principle[2] as the question whether there are *other* rules or principles which do not mention love, what their status is, and how they are related to love (whether this is conceived as a principle or not). . . . Some take faith or commitment to God as the basic virtue or posture of Christian ethics, rather than love, but even then most of what I say will hold with "faith" or "commitment to God" substituted where I say "love".'[3]

Pure Agapism, which allows no *basic* ethical principles other than or independent of love,[4] may take *four* forms:

(*a*) *Pure Act-Agapism*. This view holds that 'one is to discover or decide what one's right or duty in a particular situation is solely by confronting one's loving will with the facts of that situation . . .'.[5] The facts of other similar situations, or generalisations drawn from such situations, or from previous moments of loving obedience, are simply irrelevant or misleading. This is 'circumstance' or 'situational' ethics in its purest form. This view, of course, may be formulated without using '*agapé*': it holds that 'each moral decision about what to do is to be a direct function of faith, . . . or the experience of God together with a knowledge of the facts of the case, with no other ethical principles coming into the matter'.[6]

(*b*) *Summary Rule Agapism* or *Modified Act-Agapism*. Here I deliberately reverse the sequence of Frankena's two expressions

[1] p. 208.
[2] Frankena has already specified (p. 206) that, while a distinction between a 'rule' and a 'principle' may be important in some contexts, he proposes to use these words interchangeably in the present context.
[3] p. 206.   [4] p. 208.   [5] p. 211.   [6] p. 205.

94

for this position, in order to emphasise and make more prominent its reliance on 'summary rules'. This view holds that there are rules of conduct. These rules are summaries of past experience, perhaps of past acts of loving obedience; but 'it cannot allow that a rule [or principle] may ever be followed in a situation when it seems to conflict with what love dictates in that situation. For, if rules are to be followed only in so far as they are helpful as aids to love, they cannot constrain or constrict love in any way.'[1] We have had an example of this position under scrutiny in so far as Robinson modifies his act-agapism to include a considerable concern for 'working rules' or in so far as his 'working rules' are not intended and cannot be shown to be rules that have general validity. Frankena himself says that perhaps some of the so-called contextualists or 'circumstance' moralists actually belong in this category; and he cites Joseph Sittler's *The Structure of Christian Ethics*[2] as an example.

(c) *Pure Rule-Agapism.* This view maintains that 'we are always to tell what we are to do in particular situations by referring to a set of rules, and that what rules are to prevail and be followed is to be determined by seeing what rules (not what acts) best or most fully embody love'.[3]

To these three types of pure agapism it should at once be added that there is a fourth classification:

(d) *Combinations* of Act-Agapism and Rule-Agapism[4]; or combinations of Act-Agapism, Summary Rule Agapism and Rule-Agapism. *Vide*: John A. T. Robinson. This final type of pure agapism arises from the fact that Act-Agapism may be believed to apply in certain kinds of particular cases or situations while Rule-Agapism applies to other kinds of situations or moral problems.[5] (Someone *might* say, for example, that Act-Agapism or its modification into Summary Rule Agapism govern private morality, while Pure Rule Agapism to a very great extent governs public morality or social ethics.) Combinations also arise from the fact that Summary Rule Agapism may be believed to be the correct interpretation of certain principles of conduct, while Pure Rule Agapism is required for

[1] p. 212.   [2] Baton Rouge, Louisiana: L.S.U. Press, 1958.
[3] p. 212. Below, I shall object to the primacy given, in this description of Christian moral judgments, to 'referring to a set of rules'.
[4] p. 214.
[5] cf. p. 208 for this assertion about utilitarianism.

95

an adequate understanding of certain other principles.[1] It would seem, in fact, that if a Christian ethicist is going to be a Pure Agapist he would find this fourth possibility to be the most fruitful one, and most in accord with the freedom of *agapé* both to act through the firmest principles and to act if need be without them.

Let us at this point call a halt in our exposition of Frankena's types in order to pose for ourselves as well as for him some exceedingly important questions.

In introducing this typology in his book on *Ethics*, Frankena seemed to locate Agapism as a possible normative ethical theory between or beyond *teleology* and *deontology*. The reference to act and rule-utilitarianism (which is the prime example of teleological ethics in the modern period) was only an analogy to aid in the construction of the sub-types. His own view was, it is true, that *agapé* should be identified with 'the principle of benevolence, that is, of doing good'[2]; and that meant to reduce agapism to a form of teleological ethics. That was to take away what was granted in the first place, namely, that Christian ethics may be a third type of normative theory that is neither teleology nor deontology.

In the present essay Frankena seems to me to associate agapism from the beginning even more closely with utilitarianism, with teleological ethics, or with the principle of benevolence or doing good in the sense of ends or consequences—which, of course, is his own constructive position. This is a debatable point. As the discussion of Christian ethics proceeds it will be necessary, in order to restore the balance, for a possible closer relation with deontological theories to be explored. Analogies for possible sub-types of pure agapism can also be found here: there is an act-deontology, a summary rule deontology and a pure rule deontology, as Frankena points out.[3] If agapism is *not* a third and a distinctive type of normative theory which is neither *teleology* (goal-seeking) nor *deontology* (an ethics of duty), then it seems to me more true to say that it is a type of deontology than to say that it is a type of teleology.

[1] cf. p. 221.
[2] *Ethics*, p. 44: to be supplemented (as also utilitarianism must be, according to Frankena) by a principle of distributive justice or equality.
[3] p. 209. It is on this page that Frankena begs the question about the teleological orientation of *agapé* when he brings in deontology in the course of showing that Christian 'schemes of morality need not be wholly agapistic'.

Agapé defines for the Christian what is right, righteous, obliga-
tory to be done among men; it is not a Christian's definition of
the good that better be done and much less is it a definition of
the right way to the good. This is a fundamental problem that
has hardly begun to be debated among Christian ethicists,
since it is generally supposed, without that cogent and rigorous
argument for which he calls, that Frankena's opinion about love
and the principle of benevolence must be correct.

Eschatology has at least this significance for Christian ethics
in all ages: that reliance on producing *teloi* or on doing good
consequences or on goal-seeking has been decisively set aside.
The meaning of obligation or of right action is not to be
derived from any of these ends in view in an age that is fast
being liquidated. The Christian understanding of righteousness
is therefore radically non-teleological. It means ready obedience to the *present* reign of God, the alignment of the human
will with the Divine will that men should live together in
covenant-love no matter what the morrow brings, or if it brings
nothing. When Christ comes he will ask whether there is any
faith and love in the earth, not whether there is any practice
of 'the principle of benevolence, i.e. doing good'.

Of course, after the waning of the Christian expectation of
an early end and when the years continued to come without
ceasing one after another, this understanding of righteousness
took on the character of doing good in the sense that the results
of any action should be calculated for as far ahead as the mind
can see. Maintaining the social order, and later reconstructing
it, replaced the giving of a cup of cold water as more significant
ways to exhibit righteousness. But these are still witnessing
actions. They manifest covenant-righteousness, or make this
more possible among men. The benefits of these actions, the
good they do, is a *service*; it is never a *reliance* in the Christian
life. Therefore Christian normative ethics cannot primarily be
a type of teleology. It cannot derive its notion of what's right
from a notion of what's good, or from goals that are worth
seeking. A teleological calculus (no matter how *ideal*) can be
included in Christian ethics only in the service of its definition of
righteousness, and subordinate to its view of obedient love.
Whether this means that Christian ethics is a form of deontology, or a third type of normative theory that is neither deontology nor teleology, remains unresolved. But the reduction of

97

Christian ethics to teleology is nearly the same thing as abandoning it.

A second set of basic questions that should be raised concerns the nature of the decision in Christian ethics (if choice must be made) between Summary Rule and Pure Rule Agapism.[1] If one takes the latter viewpoint, he must say, for example:

'Keeping-promises-always is love-fulfilling.'

This will be a principle that has general validity even if it is a derived or secondary principle. It is one of those 'classes of things' of which Bishop Robinson said that it is so inconceivable they could ever express love that for the Christian they can never be right. Breaking-promises is wrong however, *for this reason*, that it is never love-fulfilling. Moreover, love itself has entered and will continue to enter into the determination of the meaning of the promise-keeping that is enjoined because this will always be love-fulfilling, even as it helps to define the meaning of the prohibited breaches of promise which can never express love.

In contrast, Summary Rule Agapism will say:

'Keeping promises is "generally" love-fulfilling.'[2] The difference, according to Frankena, is that according to Pure Rule Agapism 'we may and sometimes must obey a rule in a particular situation even though the action it calls for is seen not to be what love itself would directly require'[3]; while proponents of Summary Rule Agapism 'cannot allow that a rule may ever be followed in a particular situation when following it is known not to have the best possible [or love-fulfilling] consequences in this particular case'.[4]

[1] Pure Act Agapism seems to be a possibility only because a good many people think the unexamined life is worth living!

[2] On p. 212 of this essay, Frankena opposes 'Keeping promises is always love-fulfilling' (Summary Rule) to 'Keeping-promises-always is love-fulfilling' (Pure Rule Agapism). The first formulation does not seem to be correct. If the word 'always' means what it says, there is little difference between the first and the second formulation. I correct this and also Frankena's rule for Summary Rule Utilitarianism ('Keeping promises is always for the greatest general good'). This correction is supported by the line two lines above that utilitarian formulation (on p. 208), where Frankena writes: 'it is *always or generally* for the greatest good to act in a certain way in such situations' (italics added); and by the contrast he draws between 'Telling the truth is *generally* for the greatest good' and 'Our *always* telling the truth is for the greatest good', in his *Ethics*, p. 31.

[3] p. 212.

[4] p. 208. In the text above I criticise Frankena's statement of the Pure Rule position as a model for a possible form of Agapism. In addition to this it may be observed that the Pure Rule theory, as this is debated among philosophers, has affinity, and perhaps consanguinity, with an argument in utilitarianism that not only set up 'the general happiness' as the criterion but also presupposed a 'general

This draws the contrast too sharply, and in a way that would require a Christian to govern his actions if by rules at all by summary rules only, since he should always do what love requires. Perhaps those Christian ethicists who endorse acts or summary rules only have a similar if inarticulate understanding of the nature of Pure Rule Agapism. To correct Frankena will be to correct them also. It will be to join the issue where it should be joined; and, possibly in some combination of Summary and Pure Rule Agapism, to establish the fact that *Pure* Agapism may take two possible forms each of which *equally* may be expressions of love in that very decision to be made, i.e. in the novel and exceptional or in the ruled action to be performed. There may be kinds of situations or kinds of principles in which love implies rules summarising love's past obedience or experience and there may be situations or principles in which love implies rules that have general validity. The discussion is prejudiced from the very beginning if Pure Rule Agapism is defined in such fashion that this means that a Christian should obey a rule 'even though the action it calls for is seen not to be what love itself would directly require'. That would be to do less or something other than love requires.

I cannot speak for the pure rule utilitarian, or for how philosophers are accustomed to speak about rules. But the Christian does not believe that he lives in a world populated by rules, or that there is a 'general subject' of moral agency acting in accord with these rules, or that he should tell what he should do in particular situations (as Frankena seems to suggest) *by referring to a set of rules* and choosing from among them those that are to be followed by seeing what rules best or most fully embody love.[1]

subject' to will it according to the rules of utility. '. . . We have not only all the proof which the case admits of', wrote J. S. Mill (*Utilitarianism*, ch. iv), 'but all which it is possible to require, that happiness is a good: that each person's happiness is a good to that person, and the general happiness, therefore, a good to the aggregate of persons.' I am not now concerned with Mill's error in supposing that good = desired = desirable, but with the two tracks along which desire runs: (1) one person—his happiness; (2) 'the aggregate of persons'—the general happiness. On this view there are bound to be rules which embody *the general will's* way of aiming at general happiness which should always be obeyed *by the generality* even though the action these rules call for is seen not to be directly required by the principle of utility in an individual's calculus of *his* happiness. Pure Rule Agapism, to the contrary, will be a matter of each person doing what love requires or, if you please, himself willing generally, and therefore the rules (if rules there are) will *be* what love requires.

[1] cf. p. 212.

The Pure Rule Agapist does not follow the rule thus selected even when he knows very well that this leads to particular actions that do not embody love as well as would other actions that he might have performed.

Pure Rule Agapism, if there is such a position in Christian normative ethics, proceeds rather the other way around. It begins with persons and then devolves or discerns the rules. And yet, I believe, it can and may and must arrive at more than summary rules. There is such a thing as Pure Rule Agapism, and this covers a good part of the moral decisions and problems in the midst of which the Christian life must find its direction. The Christian—and this includes the Pure Rule Agapist—starts with people and not rules. He starts with the multiple claims and needs of his neighbours for whom Christ died. If then, among the directives in which love manifests its direction and service there are any that are discovered to have general validity, this would precisely mean that when a man omits to act in accord with these rules or principles or when he acts contrary to them he would fail to do what love requires in that situation and would act contrary to the requirement of love in that situation. Starting with persons in all the actuality of their concrete beings (but without the blinkers of moment-alism on his eyes), a Christian with unswerving compassion asks: What does love require? It is indifferent whether this leads to particular acts and summary rules only or also to general principles of conduct. If love leads to them, it leads to them. A Christian should still do what love requires.

If it could be shown that to act in accord with one of these love-formed principles of conduct is in a particular situation not what love itself directly requires, then that was not a general principle of conduct but a summary rule only. A Christian, however, will be particularly careful lest for 'what love directly requires' he has put 'what love (or sentiment) *immediately* requires'; and he foreknows that such unruly be-haviour may not be what love requires.

This is the only way to *join* the issue between Summary Rule and Pure Rule Agapism; and it is the only way for there to be any collaboration between them in the whole of Christian ethics. The question is simply whether there *are* any general rules or principles or virtues or styles of life that embody love, and if so what these may be? Answers that have been given to this question include the characteristics of love peerlessly set forth in I Corinthians 13 (which are all, so far as I can see, *universal* statements about what *agapé* requires); the qualities called the 'fruits' or 'works' and 'gifts' of the Spirit by St. Paul; the qualities called theological virtues, infused moral virtues, gifts, fruits and Beatitudes in Thomistic ethics; what Christ teaches us concerning the broadest and deepest meaning of justice; the bond of marriage tempered to the meaning and strength indicated in Ephesians 5; order or the orders in dialectical relation with justice and with love; truth-telling and promise-keeping; and (as the floor below which love can and may and must not fall) those works of sin in the flesh listed in Scripture, the more or less than seven more or less deadly sins, or those 'classes of things' like murder, theft, rape, promiscuity, pillage, adultery and sexual relations that are genuinely and therefore irresponsibly pre-marital. Some of these things may not be quite general, and there may be more to be added that will always and everywhere form the conscience and the life of the Christian man.[1] But the point to be made in an essay on the methods of ethics is simply that Pure Rule Agapism cannot be ruled out once its definition is corrected as I have suggested. To do so, or to accept Frankena's definition it (which is that of a legalism that does less than love requires) would be like saying that love cannot will in every situation what in fact it does will to do or not to do. Doubtless what *agapé* requires can always be resolved into what love finds itself required to do, and what is pleasing to love can be resolved into what love ever finds it pleasing to do (if that is proper speaking). But to rule out from this any concern for general principles of conduct (or to say that in following these rules love's concrete requirements are violated) arbitrarily limits the freedom of love in determining the right. It says that 'Love, and do as you *then* please' can mean almost anything, *except* that it *cannot* mean that anything will be found to be generally pleasing. Of course, the Rule Agapist says that one ought not act wide of the rule *for this reason*, because of the love that is in it and which would be violated by any departure from it. But this is only for him to invoke or fall back upon his most basic theory of normative ethics. This does not make him

---

[1] I would add the *agapé koinonia* ethics concerning justice in war and in the use of political power generally.

a situationalist who does not know beforehand this much, and very much else, about the requirements of love. Nor does he expect ever to support action in accord with rules even though they can be 'seen' to mean doing in a particular situation less than love requires. *He sees no such thing,* and that is why he is a proponent of Pure Rule Agapism in some matters.

One final and a related point. This has to do with the openness of Act Agapism, or a situational ethic that is truly based on *agapé* and not upon some other foundation, to the fashioning of rules of conduct. The point to be made is that Act Agapism drives on to Rule Agapism of some sort, just as we have shown in the above that Summary Rule drives on or is open to Pure Rule Agapism as part of the truth to be discerned by the Christian.

At one point Frankena describes pure act-utilitarianism in a way to which we must take strong exception, if this was meant to hold also for its analogue in Christian ethical theory. '. . . One is to tell', Frankena writes, 'what is one's right or duty in a particular situation simply by an appeal to the principle of utility, that is, by looking to see what action will produce or probably produce the greatest balance of good over evil, counting all of the consequences which it itself causes or will probably cause and no others, and in particular ignoring the consequences which might be brought about if the same thing were done in similar situations (i.e. if it were made a rule to do that act in such situations)'.[1] Because of the limitation that statement (perhaps correctly) places—in its latter portion—upon how a utilitarian should count the consequences, Frankena himself believes that the principle of benevolence or doing good has to be supplemented by an independent principle of just distribution or equality. Certainly a proponent of Act Agapism should take exception to any such description of his position in ethics, not because *agapé* is in need of supplement but because it contains in itself the corrective of the individualism of this calculus of doing good. Act Agapism, if it is truly grounded in *agapé*, cannot remain content with restricting its concern to the *direct* consequences of its own single action. I grant that Frankena's statement may be logically quite exact as also a formulation of Act-Agapism, in excluding consideration of any *explicit* rule that men should act generally as the Agapist acts unusually. The statement itself would be difficult for the Act

[1] p. 207.

Agapist to object to. He would not know, for example, whether to *deny* that he means to ignore the consequences which might be brought about if the same thing were done in similar situations (the *indirect* consequences of his action and example upon the accepted ethic), or whether to *enlarge* the conception of the consequences of his action that are to be counted to include those indirectly caused or occasioned by his action. But one way or another the Christian will know that an exceptional action of his (which may be the most loving thing to do in all its own *direct* consequences and probable consequences) may still as a side-effect tend to break down the social practice of a rule of behaviour which 'generally' embodies love and thus lead in the end and on balance to a totality of less loving actions than if he had not made an exception of himself and his single action (which, however, it cannot be denied, *was* justified in terms of an individualistic act-calculus). This is just to say that even the Christian who thinks of himself as an Act Agapist has or should have an *implicit* concern for the social consequences that are not in the direct line of his action for the social fabric in which all men must dwell, for the most fellow-ship-producing general rules of action. Thus does *agapé* in the form of Act-Agapism drive on and open the way to Summary Rule Agapism, and the *agapé* at work in summary rules drives on and opens the way, so far as may be, to Pure Rule Agapism. This for Christian ethics is the meaning of being ready for Jesus Christ to reign over human life and the meaning of being ready to do everything that love requires—everything without a single exception (not even excepting general rules).

At this point it may be pertinent to insert a comment upon the notion of 'order' or 'the orders' in Christian social ethics. This motion cannot but be puzzling to a philosopher who does ethics in terms that are all exclusively *ethical*, as the notion of 'order' or 'the orders' seems not to be. Yet (and despite the fact that the notion of 'the orders' in any profound system Christian ethics is a complex one containing more than one ingredient) this is also a form of rule-governing love. Christian ethics does not get to the notion of 'the orders' exclusively through the concept of justice, as philosophical ethics tends to do. It does not prize order simply for the justice there may be in it; or begin to upset order or withdraw its moral warrant at the point where injustice appears. Order is not only for the sake of justice. Instead, in some measure justice is also for the sake of order, since a social order can only endure so long as men adhere to it or love it for the degree of justice there is in it. They will not sustain order unless there is a tolerable justice. Therefore justice is for the sake of order as well as order for the sake of justice. Order and justice are both 'values'; both are rules of love. Order may be a conditional value and justice a higher value; but order is not merely menial in the service of justice. Order is a good in itself, in that the orders provide the fabric in which men may dwell. This means that no Christian, not even an Act Agapist if he is at all sensitive to the concrete requirements of love, should justify a revolution (violent *or non-violent*) in the social order simply or only because a greater justice belongs also among the requirements of love. Habits of upheaval and disobedience to law on one's own determination that it is unjust are not easily slacked. Order and justice are dialectically related rules of love; and a Christian will be alert to the indirect consequences of even those acts of his that are motivated by a loving justice in destroying the accepted ethic, the rules of social due process, the social habit of compliance with law, etc.

I should say that this wisdom was forgotten by a great many of the leaders of Christian opinion and action in the United States during our national ordeal of the struggle for greater inter-racial justice, who substituted for it the categories of a dynamic secular idealism with its resultant utopianism and Manichaeanism (the Negro 'revolution', the 'white power structure', the 'struggle', 'direct action', 'an unjust law is no law at all') which no Christian should let become primary in his view of social relations. If it is *agapé* and not something else masquerading under this label that is at work seeking to discover all that love requires, there will be an inner pressure within acts that seek to be concretely loving also toward order (and not only order so far as it is just) as among the fundamental needs of men. This too will be seen to be among the rules of love that are generally valid. An act that goes wide of this rule because it is 'seen' to be the most love-fulfilling thing to do can only seem so. Order is a provision of Pure Rule Agapism that has general validity; and, within this, obedience to law is certainly a summary rule.

I should say that the exceptional disobedience to law, if it is properly surrounded and located by all that love requires, is to be inversely determined by the possibilities in social due process and in the momentum of the social forces for reforming or changing that law; and that from the beginning of the current civil rights movement in the United States the duty of compliance with law has been vastly underestimated by many of the leaders of Christian opinion and action. People often say that social disorganisation is only a symptom of injustice and of the alienation and resentment that results from this. But when society becomes dis-ordered it will not be *only* for lack of justice. This will also be because of a lack of respect for the value of order itself, for the majesty of political rulership as such, and for the service of human life these things perform. And this in turn will be not only because the 'worse elements' (the *Lumpenproletariat*) fall below obedience to social due process and the compliance required for social peace and required by a consideration for the unadjudicated and still legal rights of others. It will also, and especially in the modern liberal period, be because the 'better elements' aspire too highly (or too narrowly) in taking the sole standard and goal of community life to be 'at the same time the free expression of the individual and ... absolute social cohesion' (which was J. L. Tolman's definition of utopianism).

It is time now for us to get back on Frankena's track.

2. *Mixed Agapism*

There may be theologians who regard love as *one* of the principles to be used in the elaboration of Christian ethics, but not as the only basic one. Such a normative theory of ethics Frankena calls 'mixed agapism', in contrast to the types of pure agapism that we have so far considered. For views of this second sort there are judgments about right and wrong which are independent of love and of love derived rules or acts. It is important that Mixed Agapism not be restricted to theories that combine agapism with natural or rational morality. This type says only that there *are* principles or precepts that are *not* derived from the law of love in any such way as pure agapists believed to be the nature and source of all their principles. Such non-agapistic norms may be known to us from *revelation* no less than there may be norms that are naturally known.[1]

[1] p. 216.

The conclusion that either is also basic within Christian ethics would produce an instance of Mixed Agapism. Frankena takes C. H. Dodd's *Gospel and Law*[1] to illustrate this; and he is correct if Dodd believes that there are 'ethical precepts' in the Gospels which are neither the summary nor the general rules of love but which still govern the Christian life. The conservative Christian ethics written in America by Carl F. H. Henry[2] would be another example. So also would Bonhoeffer's doctrine of the biblical 'mandates' (even if one would never gain this impression from the purveyors of Bonhoeffer in the English speaking world).[3] Thus, theories of divine law as well as theories of Christian natural law may be classified under Mixed Agapism.

Still, theories of the 'Christian natural law' and an ethics of the 'orders of creation' are the more usual examples of what Frankena calls Mixed Agapism. Perhaps an American theologian can say what few Protestant theologians on the continent of Europe can yet say concerning these possibilities; so let me now say it. In the discussion of Christian ethical principles of explanation and interpretation, it is high time we returned to a bit of wisdom that is so old the Latins had a word for it: *abusus non tollit usum*. Of course, the 'German Christians' grossly abused the notion that in part God's will may be immanent

[1] p. 223, n. 24. If the Christian ethicist wants to begin at the beginning and with the 'given' in Christian ethics, he will have systematically to come to terms with W. D. Davies' *The Context of the Sermon on the Mount* (Cambridge, England: The University Press, 1964). Taking into account the fact that this admirable study is an historical work and not as such a constructive statement of Christian ethics, the evidence Professor Davies gathers and the reasonable interpretation he gives of the foundational New Testament documents comes close to excluding Act Agapism from among positions in Christian ethics on the part of anyone who wants to be faithful to the Source and to the sources of our faith. Whether Pure Rule Agapism receives the more support from this study, or some form of Mixed Agapism (there being authoritative teachings of the Christ that are not reducible to forms or expressions of love)—this question I will simply place on the agenda.

[2] *Christian Personal Ethics*. Grand Rapids, Michigan: Wm. B. Eerdmans Publishing Co., 1957.

[3] It is possible, of course, that both Henry and Bonhoeffer are instances of *non*-agapism (or of *derived* agapism), depending on the degree of primacy and independence assigned to love in their systems. For that matter, if love is at all a source of the Christian life for Bonhoeffer, he may be a *mixed* agapist—although, again, no one is apt to gain the impression from the purveyors of Bonhoeffer in the English speaking world that he actually makes extensive use of a category of the 'unnatural' or the 'inhumane' in his probing description of man's plight in this world that has come of age. Moreover, the disciples of Bonhoeffer in the United States do not grapple with him in the matter of his 'special ethics' (which often contains some quite conservative opinions)—no more than Lehmann deserves to be called a Barthian (or a learner from him) so long as he ignores Barth's doctrines of creation and man and the 'special ethics' built on this.

within the created order. So also did the divine-right monarchs grossly abuse the notion that God's will is extrinsic and comes from above to impose righteousness upon the world. To correct the one abuse the Confessing Church appealed to the sovereignty of God over the entire creation, and to correct the other abuse Calvinists of the left-wing appealed to an immanent justice in support of wars of civil and religious liberty. In any case, *abusus non tollit usum*, and history settles nothing.

Protestant theological ethics will hardly set its house in order until it learns this lesson, and begins to debate issues without prejudice. What, for example, are we to make of the efforts present-day theologians make to avoid at all cost the use of the word 'orders' while saying the same thing by means of a different term that should puzzle any reader to tell the difference? Thus, at the outset of his 'special ethics', Karl Barth speaks of the 'contours' of the event or field of obedience, and of a 'formed reference' to the ethical event. The reader has reason to suppose that these are Christologically penetrated orders of creation until Barth disavows this. Or does he? Does he *succeed* in doing so merely by saying so?—when he writes: 'These might very well be called *orders* or *ordinances*. But then there would always be the possibility of misunderstanding them as laws, prescriptions and imperatives. They are *spheres* in which God commands and man is obedient or disobedient. . . .'[1] There where Dietrich Bonhoeffer introduces his discussion of the 'mandates of God in the world', which He imposes on all men, we are suddenly warned that something terribly important is at stake in *not* calling these 'orders': 'We speak of divine mandates rather than of divine orders because the word mandate refers most clearly to a divinely imposed task rather than a determination of being.'[2] Who does not know that Emil Brunner's 'orders' are divinely imposed tasks rather than determinations of being, that they are orders of God's governance of the world rather than orders of created being apart from the Creator, Governor, Preserver and Redeemer of the world?

There remain legitimate and important differences among these systems of theological ethics, but these differences are confused and not focused by all this effort to avoid using the word 'order' or even 'order of creation'. The question is not

[1] *Church Dogmatics* III, 4, §52, pp. 29-30 (italics added).
[2] *Ethics*, p. 73.

the usefulness or the need for these categories in any full elaboration of Christian ethics. The question to be debated is rather whether the 'orders' are to be understood only Christologically (Pure Agapism) or *also* in some degree by natural reason (Mixed Agapism). The latter possibility would seem to be entailed in the conviction that when Christ came He came to 'His own'.

3. *Non-Agapism*

Finally Frankena introduces a third generic type. For him to do so may be somewhat inconsistent with his earlier statements that seemed to use the term *agapé* in such a large and loose sense that it was said either that this includes 'faith' or 'the experience of God' or 'God's commands', etc. as primary ethical categories or that an ethics that uses any such primary ethical term in place of *agapé* would be productive of the same typology as the one Frankena elaborates by means of this root word. Still it may be important for us to take note of the fact that Frankena finds in the literature of Christian ethics normative theories that make use of 'the imitation of God' or 'gratitude to God', etc. to refer to the primary posture of the Christian life and the primary norm to be used in Christian ethical reflection and seem not to use the term 'love' at all, or at all significantly. These views he calls Non-Agapism.

Some of these views, however, may use the norm of love *derivatively*. For example, A. C. Garnett's normative theory is self-realisation, but Christian agapism tells him the way this can and may and must be accomplished. This is an example[1] of *derived agapism* within a non-agapistic normative theory. So also a working or derived agapism may be the way to obey God's commands or imitate Him or show gratitude or do His will.

It may be long past time to call a halt to Frankena's inventions. But since our purpose is the preparation of an agenda for the possible clarification of the tasks and methods of Christian ethics, we ought finally to note a few of Frankena's notations concerning certain celebrated and less than cele-

[1] p. 218.

108

brated Christian theologians he has read who are doing ethics today.

Emil Brunner's position, Frankena writes, 'seems to me to be quite ambiguous; sometimes it looks like a form of act-agapism, but at others like a form of mixed agapism or even like a species of non-agapism'.[1] As for Reinhold Niebuhr, 'he appears to me to suggest, in one place or another, almost every one of the positions I have described; whether this spells richness or confusion of mind I shall leave for others to judge'.[2] 'Paul Ramsey . . . has been attacking such theories [pure act-agapism] lately, but in *Basic Christian Ethics* he appeared to come very close to agreeing with them.'[3] 'Presumably what Ramsey calls "in-principled love-ethics" falls under one of [the forms of rule-agapism], but I have not been able to tell which.'[4] 'I have mentioned Ramsey, but am not clear just what his position is. It seems to be a form of pure agapism—or possibly of derived agapism—but it is not clear just what kind of pure agapism it is and it may even be a kind of impure or mixed agapism.'[5]

None of the above mentioned writers ought too readily to reply that Frankena's puzzlement only shows that his typology is too abstract and therefore not suited to the purpose of enabling him the better to see the meaning of Christian ethics.

As for myself, I have already indicated that if one is going to be a proponent of Pure Agapism, it would seem that some combination [1(d) above] of Act-Agapism, Summary Rule and Pure Rule Agapism will prove the most fruitful procedure and theory to explore in regard to the situations, moral problems or principles that may turn out to be corrigible to adequate interpretation by one or another of these procedures within the normative ethic of Pure Agapism.

It remains for me to say that, on account of the diversity in the practical wisdom that may be needed for the guidance of moral and political action, it seems to me that if a Christian ethicist is going to be so far a Pure Agapist, and as far as this will take him in throwing light upon the path of action, still there can be no sufficient reason for him programmatically to exclude the possibility that there may be rules, principles or precepts whose source is man's natural competence to make

[1] p. 220.   [2] p. 220.
[3] pp. 211-12.   [4] p. 214.
[5] p. 219.

moral judgments.[1] An inhabitant of Jerusalem need not rely on messages from Athens, but he should not refuse them; and he might even go to see if there are any. This would be Mixed Agapism—a combination of *agapé* with man's sense of natural justice or injustice which, however, contains an internal asymmetry that I indicate by the expression 'love transforming natural justice'.[2]

[1] This says nothing about *how* and *why* love leads to principles or *how* and *why* natural moral knowledge arises. These questions come much later on the agenda; and they may fall within meta-ethics, and not at all within normative ethics. For the record, I will only indicate that Frankena (pp. 213-14) makes some interesting remarks upon the question *why* 'love is thus constrained to express itself through rules or principles rather than by doing in each case the act which is most loving in that case'.

[2] See my *Nine Modern Moralists* (Englewood Cliffs, New Jersey: Prentice-Hall, Inc., 1962) and *Christian Ethics and the Sit-In* (New York: The Association Press 1961), esp. pp. 124-8. I do not see how Frankena can conclude that my *Basic Christian Ethics* (New York: Chs. Scribner's Sons, 1950) exhibited in the whole of it the position of Act Agapism. True, that book was concerned to clarify what I regard to be both *primary* and also *distinctive* in Christian ethics. I freely concede that *agapé* itself was so analysed as to leave standing the assumption that this could itself come to full and faithful expression in acts only, and never in rules also; and that such principles, moral bonds and structures as there may be would derive from some source secondary to this. But to say that only *agapé* is primary and distinctive does not deny that there may be independent secondary and non-distinctive principles (Mixed Agapism). That book not only allowed for this possibility in what was said about '*enlightened* disinterestedness', and (as to the source of such enlightenment) in the stated indifference, so far as the primacy of *agapé* is concerned, between whether love finds that there are only social case studies to compile in telling what to do or finds that there are principles of the natural law. It only denied that natural justice is not primary or distinctive in Christian ethics, thus putting natural justice, if there are such principles, in the quite secondary position where it may be subject to elevation and transformation by love. The book also made generous use of the principle of generalisation in ethics and of the truth to be drawn from idealistic social philosophy in elaborating a Christian social policy.

Scottish Journal of Theology Occasional Papers No. 11